T0146419

WATKINS TAPSELL'S
GUIDE TO SEPARATION AND FAMILY LAW

OR, EVERYTHING YOU NEED TO KNOW BEFORE
YOU DIVORCE BUT ARE AFRAID TO ASK

MATTHEW COATES, KRISTY DURRANT & JAMIE ROCHE

BALBOA.
PRESS

A DIVISION OF HAY HOUSE

Balboa Press books may be ordered through booksellers or by contacting:

Balboa Press
A Division of Hay House
1663 Liberty Drive
Bloomington, IN 47403
www.balboapress.com.au
1 (877) 407-4847

Because of the dynamic nature of the Internet, any web addresses or links contained in this book may have changed since publication and may no longer be valid. The views expressed in this work are solely those of the author and do not necessarily reflect the views of the publisher, and the publisher hereby disclaims any responsibility for them.

The author of this book does not dispense medical advice or prescribe the use of any technique as a form of treatment for physical, emotional, or medical problems without the advice of a physician, either directly or indirectly. The intent of the author is only to offer information of a general nature to help you in your quest for emotional and spiritual well-being. In the event you use any of the information in this book for yourself, which is your constitutional right, the author and the publisher assume no responsibility for your actions.

Any people depicted in stock imagery provided by Thinkstock are models, and such images are being used for illustrative purposes only.
Certain stock imagery © Thinkstock.

Print information available on the last page.

ISBN: 978-1-5043-0505-1 (sc)
ISBN: 978-1-5043-0506-8 (e)

Balboa Press rev. date: 11/25/2016

CONTENTS

CHAPTER 1

HOW DO YOU SEPARATE?

Chapter Summary

In this chapter, we aim to guide you through the process of the initial separation and show you how to commence discussions with your former partner to resolve all the issues arising from a relationship breakdown. The lessons to be discussed in this chapter are as follows:

Lesson 1—Identify and Open Up to Your Support Network at the Start of the Separation Process

Lesson 2—Start the Process by Notifying Your Former Partner That the Relationship Is Over

Lesson 3—Carefully Work Out Your Post-Separation Living Arrangements with Your Support Network and Financial Advisor

Lesson 4—Tailor Your Negotiation Approach to Your Former Partner's Emotional Status

Lesson 5—Act Quickly to Protect Yourself if Faced with the Risk of Violence, and Act to Mitigate Your Risk of Being Falsely Accused of Violence

Taking the Leap

People often meet with a lawyer for the first time some months prior to their engaging that lawyer to assist them through a family law dispute. Why is there this gap? The main reason is that the decision to separate from one's partner can be an extremely difficult one with a myriad of consequences. No one takes the decision to separate lightly. In fact, the decision is quite often the culmination of months (or years) of forethought and planning. There are many things to consider and there are many things to plan, both of which we explore in this chapter.

In any scenario, making the decision to separate is a big one, and it is forever life-altering (albeit often positive). The decision to separate is akin to "taking a leap," as it requires bravery and a commitment to throw oneself into the unknown. There is no guarantee of anything. There is no safety net. You are taking a chance that your life is going to be better as a result of this dramatic life move. There are many facets of separation that need to be considered prior to taking that leap, and we have set them out in this chapter.

LESSON 1

Identify and Open Up to Your Support Network at the Start of the Separation Process

The Importance of Emotional Support

When you are starting the process of ending a relationship, one of the key factors at play is the support of loved ones and professionals. When pursuing separation, people tend to think of themselves as being isolated. They often excommunicate themselves from social groups and lose joint friendships enjoyed during the relationship. This is the opposite of what should occur. The period of separation is truly a time in which the person on the journey should reach out to, and remain connected and engaged with, the people in his or her life. While separation can be burdensome in many ways, the burden on newly separated people is substantially reduced when they have trusted people they can speak to. Great examples of personal supports can be loved ones such as adult children, siblings, parents, friends, and even a new life partner. These familial and friend-based supports can be used to discuss the problems you are facing, provide you with informal advice, and just get your mind off things for a while.

In addition to the informal support family and friends can offer in an especially emotionally gruelling break up, you can seek out professional support to help you cope. Some examples of professional supporters are counsellors, life coaches, mentors, religious leaders, and mental health professionals, such as psychologists and psychiatrists. There can be great value to a person seeking professional support while dealing with a family relationship crisis. Lawyers are often the first professionals approached for advice, but they are not the best professionals to assist clients with the emotional and mental health aspects of their personal lives; it is simply not what lawyers are trained to do. A good lawyer will, however, identify issues and refer a client to appropriate trusted professionals who can provide mental health and/or emotional support services. In addition, it is important to know that in our social media age, there is a multitude of online support available for the newly separated, covering issues such as parenting, managing your emotions, and moving on. Before you take the first step towards implementing a separation, we recommend that you consolidate and understand your support network so that it is available when you will need to rely on it. Without that support in place, you risk an overpowering sense of isolation, which can (at best) undermine your attempts to end the relationship or (at worst), put you in a position where your ability to negotiate a sensible end to the relationship is compromised. Such a compromise can produce serious disadvantage on an emotional or a financial level.

> **Example:** Bill and Mary had been together for thirty years. Bill was a narcissist who was totally controlling throughout the relationship. Mary, who was sixty and hadn't been in the workforce for twenty years, wanted 50 per cent of their total assets. Bill didn't use a lawyer and was not giving an inch. Bill argued over everything, so Mary's legal costs were escalating. Bill believed Mary's contribution was worth only 30 per cent of the assets. Mary knew she would get 50 per cent if she went to court, but she was emotionally drained. She felt alone and worn down and just wanted out, so she accepted 30 per cent of their assets.

LESSON 2

Start the Process by Notifying Your Former Partner That the Relationship Is Over

What Is a Legal Separation?

There is a common misconception that separation is a formal process that has to be legally documented before it is valid. In reality, separation is a question of fact. If you ask yourself if you consider your relationship to be over and the answer is yes, then you are probably separated. That means you can be separated from your partner and still be living in the same house, still be sharing the responsibilities for children, and still be sharing expenses such as mortgage repayments and council rates. If you consider your relationship to have ended, you should communicate that clearly to your former partner at the outset.

Of course, there are many situations in which telling your former partner that you regard your relationship as being over is very difficult. There could be a risk of physical or emotional violence. In those circumstances, communicating the end of the relationship to your partner needs to be carefully managed in conjunction with your support network. Options for letting your former partner know of your view may include relocating away from the house before announcing your intention, announcing your intention in the presence of members of your support network, or asking your partner to leave the house while you consider your future (what is known as a *trial separation*).

LESSON 3

Carefully Work Out Your Post-Separation Living Arrangements with Your Support Network and Financial Advisor

Will You Be Disadvantaged if You Leave Your Home?

Many people believe that by leaving their home during separation, they risk suffering a legal disadvantage. Namely, they feel that by leaving the house, they are giving up their legal interest in the home or their parenting rights to the children (if the children continue to reside within the home). In reality, you will normally not be legally disadvantaged if you choose to leave your home and relocate (e.g., move in with your parents). Often, this option is the far more manageable, sensible, and amicable alternative to continuing to cohabit with your partner. There are, however, a number of practical matters to be considered before you decide to move out of the home.

If You Stay in the House

- Can you live as a separated person with your former partner under the same roof, given the emotional stress that such an arrangement can involve?
- What rules need to be agreed upon if you and your former partner are to live as separated under the same roof? These include rules covering arrangements for the children (collections from school, delivery to extracurricular activities, informing them of the separation), contributions to household expenses (including mortgage repayments), undertaking household chores, civil communication between the parties, and the timing for one of you eventually moving out.

If You Leave the House

- Will you be taking the children with you?

- What will your supervision arrangements be for the children when they are with you?
- Where will you live?
- Can you afford new accommodation (rent, bond, moving expenses, furniture)?
- Can you afford living expenses?
- Are you entitled to pension benefits, child support, or spouse maintenance?
- Do you have relatives who can provide short-term financial assistance?
- Are you able to find employment?

> **Example:** Kevin leaves Amanda in their home and takes the two children under ten with him. Amanda would not allow Kevin to take the children's bedroom furniture. Kevin rents a two-bedroom unit. Without telling Amanda, Kevin draws down on their mortgage redraw facility to fund the rental bond and the purchase of furniture and white goods. With the help of a friend, Kevin arranges to move the children's furniture from the house while Mary is at work.

If you leave your home with the children, or if you leave and have no children, then it is likely that your former partner will become solely responsible for the ongoing costs of maintaining the home (mortgage, rates, insurance, etc.) because he or she will have the benefit of sole occupation of that home. If you have children and leave the home by yourself (where the children remain in the home with your former partner), you may have to contribute to the cost of maintaining the home (mortgage, rates, insurance, etc.). Your obligation to contribute will depend largely on the comparative financial position of you and your former partner. As part of your separation planning, you should consult with a financial advisor to see what the financial impact of your relocation from the house will be and whether it is a financially viable option for you.

LESSON 4

Tailor Your Negotiation Approach to Your Former Partner's Emotional Status

Where Are You, and Where Is Your Former Partner, Situated in the Separation Process?

The Emotional Journey

One of the questions that we hear most often as family law lawyers is, "How do you deal with the emotions of your cases on a daily basis?" That is a good question, one that we will address in this chapter and often throughout *Watkins Tapsell's Guide to Separation and Family Law*. Emotions are part and parcel of family law, and it is impossible to disassociate them from your involvement in a relationship breakdown. It is not an understatement to say that a person going through separation, and the consequences that flow from it, is quite likely going through one of the worst periods of his or her life.

When we consider what happens in a separation, it is not hard to understand why it is so emotionally hard on people. Their once loving relationship has ended, which in fact can bring about significant feelings of personal failure. They are each about to lose ownership of a significant portion of their acquired wealth. Whenever an interest in 100 per cent of anything is being cut down, it can be a difficult pill to swallow. They are losing time with their children, because separated parents cannot spend the same amount of time with their children when the children are divided between two households. The former couple's vision of their future has been irreparably changed; where there was once a vision of an intact family unit sharing travels and heading into retirement, there is now uncertainty. Uncertainty breeds fear, and fear can manifest itself as negative emotions, which carry over into the family law dispute. On a lesser scale, separated couples are losing mutual friends, valued possessions, and even access to family pets (it seems low on the priority list next to everything else, but we have seen situations where custody of the family dog became a significant issue!).

What is the emotional journey to which we refer? *Emotional journey* is a phrase we use to describe the process that starts when a person considers that his or her relationship may be ending and generally concludes when that person has completed the legal process associated with the separation, accepted the end of the relationship, and moved on with his or her life. (This is not always the end point, because for some, the emotional journey can continue for a much longer period, for example, when there are ongoing parenting issues.) Your lawyer must understand this emotional minefield, as the lawyer's ability to understand an individual's emotions, and to understand how they impact the family law negotiations, is essential to bringing about a sensible early resolution. While lawyers are generally not trained psychologists, a good lawyer can empathise with, and potentially redirect, the client's emotions in a way that promotes an effective resolution.

Your Relative Positions on the Emotional Journey

A key issue for any person to understand before he or she can effectively commence negotiations with his or her former partner is the relative position of each party on the emotional journey. Each person's emotional journey is different. Some relationships end in a sudden, cataclysmic, and epic meltdown. In this case, emotions are raw and fresh, and often the end of the relationship is brought about by mistrust or infidelity. Believe it or not, these kinds of cases are (thankfully) the exception and not the rule. The far more common scenario is that the relationship has undergone a long, slow death. Sometimes the parties have stayed together for many years in a bad relationship because they have not had the means or ability to end it or they were merely maintaining their relationship for the benefit of children. These kinds of separations are far more common. Most cases of separation that we encounter fall somewhere between "sudden, cataclysmic, and epic meltdown" and "long, slow death." Each type of separation will highlight different aspects of the emotional journey.

It is very rarely the case that both parties to a separation are at the same stage of that emotional journey. Usually, one partner is the catalyst for the separation and the progression of the dispute towards a final resolution. For the purposes of this exercise, we will call that person the initiator. The initiator will usually have contemplated and accepted that the relationship has ended some considerable time before notifying his or her partner. This can often result in a situation where the initiator has come to terms with the end of the relationship whereas the other party is, at the same time, taken by surprise and unable to believe or understand that the relationship is at risk. When two people are in such different emotional positions, it makes negotiations for a final resolution of issues very difficult. While the initiator will usually be ready and anxious to achieve a final resolution, and to move on with his or her life, the other party may not understand what is happening; believe that salvaging the relationship is possible; direct all of his or her efforts towards encouraging reconciliation rather than towards achieving a final resolution of the separation issues; avoid any commitment that carries with it a sense of finality; and refuse to accept sensible and commercial advice, because to do so would involve an acceptance of the end of the relationship. Often the other party is blindsided by the fact that the initiator has progressed so far with the intention to separate. The other party may have suspected that things were not good within the relationship but may have had no idea that things had *gotten that bad*. In this situation, the other party often feels surprised by the strong feelings of the initiator. That surprise is often coupled with feelings of hurt, betrayal, and failure on the part of the other party. The initiator, at this point, has come to terms emotionally with the separation and the failure of the relationship. This process, for the initiator, could have been months or years in the making. The initiator has had a head start on the emotional journey and is ready to negotiate and finalise a sensible commercial resolution to the relationship issues.

In circumstances such as this, it is often almost impossible to reach a sensible negotiated resolution quickly. This is because the other party needs to "catch up". This person's approach in the early stages of his or her own journey may lead to outbursts, ridiculous demands in negotiations, or delay tactics. This reflects that the person is, as yet, unable to come to terms with what is happening in his or her life. Most of the time, settlement cannot occur until both parties have reached the type of equilibrium that comes when there is at least some degree of joint acceptance that the relationship is irretrievable.

Adapting Your Approach to Negotiating

Once you recognise whether an emotional journey issue applies to your circumstances, you can adopt an appropriate strategy to deal with the emotional differences of the parties. Your options include postponing negotiations until emotions have settled down; avoiding direct negotiation with your former partner, attempting resolution using intermediaries (including friends, between solicitors, or via a mediator); commence court proceedings in order to force your former partner to perceive reality and then negotiate a resolution in the context of those proceedings; or undertake negotiations in a manner that avoids forcing your former partner to overtly admit that the relationship is ended.

LESSON 5

Act Quickly to Protect Yourself if Faced with the Risk of Violence, and Act to Mitigate Your Risk of Being Falsely Accused of Violence

How Do You Deal with Emotional or Physical Violence?

As we have described within this chapter, separating from your partner is a life-changing decision that is not easily made. In a relationship involving emotional or physical violence, the decision-making process concerning separation becomes even more difficult because the self-confidence and self-worth has been stripped from the victim in various ways, often over a number of years. There are patterns of abuse and emotional or physical violence that show themselves repeatedly. In an abusive relationship, the abuser often couples with someone who is weaker than he or she (either physically, emotionally, or both). The abuser then sets out to exploit the strength he or she has over his or her partner by controlling and dominating every interaction. This relationship dynamic can persist for years, even decades. There can be sporadic or even constant physical violence on the part of the abuser, which may result in direct physical harm to the victim. The physical effects of such violence may or may not be readily apparent to an independent observer, but they will be devastating to the victim nevertheless. There can be psychological and emotional violence perpetrated on the victim by the abuser. Such damage, while not as readily apparent, is no less damaging to the abuse victim. The result of enduring an abusive relationship is that the victim is stripped of his or her confidence and independence. Often, victims are not allowed to control, or sometimes even to access, the finances of the relationship. If an abusive relationship features small children, the abuser can manipulate the children in much the same way that he or she manipulates and controls the victim of the abuse.

There are various ways in which an abusive relationship complicates the victim's decision to separate from the abusive partner: A victim's decision-making ability can be negatively affected. The victim's fear of the abuser overtakes the decision-making process and can be all-consuming. A victim of abuse who has been cut off from finances will not have the same freedom to seek help as the abuser who is controlling the funds. This results in victims perceiving that they lack the financial ability to leave their partner. If the abusive relationship also involves small children, a plan to separate from an abusive partner may not take priority over ensuring that the children are safe on a day-to-day basis.

The starting point in determining how to deal with emotional or physical violence is to recognise that violence is never acceptable in the eyes of a court or the community. If faced with the risk of violence, you should immediately remove yourself from the risk and seek support from the family members and friends who make up your support network, or contact one of the many community support services for guidance and protection. Information about the relevant community support services is readily available through the federal-government-funded Family Relationship Centres around Australia (www.familyrelationships.gov. au). You can also contact your local police station to explain your fears and to seek their assistance in obtaining an apprehended violence order from a court. Local police stations usually have a domestic violence liaison officer who can guide you through the court process and also direct you to other appropriate support services.

How Do You Respond to False Accusations of Emotional or Physical Violence?

The reality of the family law system is that just being accused of emotional or physical violence can negatively impact your position. There have been many situations where allegations of emotional or physical violence were false or heavily embellished. The effect of these allegations, if they are levied against you, can be that you are, at least initially, presumed by the legal system to be guilty until proven innocent, especially in situations where children are involved, as their protection is paramount. The stain of being labelled as an abuser within the court system puts at risk your ability to contact your former partner, to spend time with your children, or even to make decisions regarding your children's welfare.

The legal expense involved in clearing your name of false or embellished accusations can be significant.

There is no foolproof way of protecting yourself against a false or embellished allegation; however, there are steps that you can take to minimise your personal risk if you think that there is the potential for these allegations. You should not engage in heated or hostile discussions with your former partner. You should have a third party present to witness important conversations or meetings with your former partner, including visitation exchanges of the children. You should communicate only in writing with your former partner (email or SMS message is a great way to have a record of the actual exchange). You should arrange for visitation exchanges to occur in public places where witnesses are plentiful.

CHAPTER 2

STARTING THE LEGAL PROCESS

Chapter Summary

In this chapter, we look beyond the initial stages of a separation and explore the steps necessary to start the legal process. The lessons to be discussed in this chapter are as follows:

Lesson 1—Confirm That Your Relationship Is One That Is Covered by Family Law

Lesson 2—Post-Separation Communication with Your Former Partner Can Be Difficult, but It Is Necessary to Achieve an Optimal Result

Lesson 3—Carefully Choose a Lawyer to Guide You through a Family Law Dispute

Lesson 4—Understand Your Legal Entitlements from the Very Beginning of Your Case

Lesson 5—Take Simple Steps to Minimise Your Own Legal Costs

Lesson 6—Be Practical, Conciliatory, and Child-Focussed When Developing a Parenting Plan with Your Former Partner

You Have Taken the Leap. Now What?

You have considered it. You have thought about it. You have pondered, wondered, worried, predicted, emoted, and deliberated. You have taken into consideration your future, your children, and their futures, and have factored in no fewer than five hundred different variables. Your decision has been made. It is time to move on from your partner. Or, your partner has considered it, has thought about it, has pondered, wondered, worried, predicted, emoted, and deliberated. Your partner has made his or her decision and now wants to move on. The leap has been taken for you; in fact, you are being pushed. Now what do you do? We have set out guidelines in this chapter for how you can start the separation process.

LESSON 1

Confirm That Your Relationship Is One That Is Covered by Family Law

Is Your Relationship Covered by Family Law?

Not every relationship falls under family law. Family law is the law of the land when it comes to marriage (which is defined, as of the date of the writing of *Watkins Tapsell's Guide to Separation and Family Law*, as between a man and a woman) and de facto relationships (which are relationships that can be heterosexual or same sex). The parties to a de facto relationship enjoy the same rights and protections under the law that married people do. They are subject to the same laws regarding splitting of property and parenting of children. Whether you are married or not is usually clear-cut. Whether your relationship is a de facto marriage is often not as clear, and in such a situation you need to consider a number of different factors in order to answer the question of whether or not it is. These factors include whether or not the parties have a child; whether or not the relationship continued for at least two years' duration; whether or not the parties lived together; whether or not the parties mixed their property, assets, or liabilities; whether or not the parties had a sexual relationship; and whether or not the parties held themselves out to the community as a couple during their relationship.

> **Example:** Chris and Sonja each had their own house. They each slept over, two nights a week, at the other's house and had three nights per week in their own house by themselves. This arrangement had been in place for two and a half years. They kept separate bank accounts and didn't mix their finances at all. They regularly attended family and social events together and were often seen holding hands in public. They had a sexual relationship. They were a de facto couple.

There are many relationships that do not fall under the scope of family law, including dating relationships, friendships, relationships between roommates or housemates, and the relationship between a paid carer and his or her charge. The odds are that if you are reading *Watkins Tapsell's Guide to Separation and Family Law*, your relationship is one that is covered by family law. If not, consider yourself lucky, put the book down, and go enjoy yourself.

LESSON 2

Post-Separation Communication with Your Former Partner Can Be Difficult, but It Is Necessary to Achieve an Optimal Result

Communicating with Your Former Partner

Communication between a newly separated pair can be difficult. Let's face it: if communication had been a strong suit between most separated people, they probably would not have separated. The better your ability to communicate after separating, the greater your prospects of achieving a sensible early resolution to your family law issues. If you find that civil communication is impossible, do not keep attempting the impossible. It is better to cease direct communication with your former partner in this situation, just to avoid escalating the conflict. In such a situation, communication can be through third parties, such as your respective lawyers. Here are some helpful tips that will facilitate better communication with your former partner early in the separation process:

- Keep it simple. Rome was not built in a day, nor will your post-separation life be. There is a possibility that your post-separation relationship will last longer than your relationship itself, especially if there are children involved. Think of the post-separation relationship as a work in progress. You will not reach the final stages during the first month you spend apart from your former partner. It is best to start with communication that is simple and geared towards things that matter: the children, your remaining financial responsibilities to each other, and finding a way forward.

- Keep it civil. Although this should go without saying, avoiding verbal jousting or cheap shots is necessary to promoting communication with a former partner. Try saying something positive about your ex to your children, or to your ex, at least once a day. Hard as it may be, it is an excellent way to enhance communication.

- Do not rehash the past. No doubt, there were many mistakes, misdeeds, or miscommunications over the course of a failed relationship. There is no benefit to bringing those past occurrences into your present relationship.

- Be discreet. If you think that your former partner is going to be happy for you because you have re-partnered with a fitness model and that you are now driving a Porsche convertible, you are probably mistaken and will, most likely, experience communication difficulties. Be discreet, leave the Porsche at home, and ask your new partner not to come with you when you pick up the kids.

- When in doubt, put it in writing. Sometimes a former partner can be so disagreeable, so difficult to deal with, and so hostile that verbal communication is made impossible. In such cases, emails, text messages, and even letters are great ways to communicate. Not only do they take the face-to-face element out of the equation, but also they serve as a written record in the event that your former partner chooses to be disagreeable in his or her dealings with you. Such written records often make for strong evidence in court.

LESSON 3

Carefully Choose a Lawyer to Guide You through a Family Law Dispute

Choosing the Right Lawyer

It is not an understatement to say that your choice of lawyer can be one of the most important choices that you make throughout the separation process. The difference in outcomes that can occur by hiring a great lawyer as opposed to hiring a bad lawyer is vast. You probably know what makes a particular family lawyer great. A great family lawyer will have a thorough knowledge of the law and will specialise in that area of law. There is nothing more dangerous than a lawyer who "dabbles" in a particular field. A dabbler might be a wonderful person, and even a good lawyer, but if he or she is on one side of a case, pitted against a specialist with specialised knowledge, then he or she will be at a disadvantage every time. A great family lawyer will be able to use his or her knowledge of the law to clearly and accurately ascertain your legal entitlements. A great family lawyer will prepare thoroughly to understand the facts and the law concerning your case. A great family lawyer will be able to use his or her understanding of your legal entitlements, and the facts of your case, to facilitate an early sensible settlement or, should that prove impossible, to craft a strong court case.

But did you know that a great family lawyer will also listen to you and understand your concerns and the interests you want to protect, even where those concerns and interests have nothing to do with the law; approach your circumstances in a sensible, problem-solving manner, uninfluenced by emotion or irrelevant factors; tell you no if you ask to take a path that is not constructive or that is not likely to lead to a positive result for you; and present you with options? On top of this, a great lawyer will be honest with you. If your case is horrible, that lawyer will tell you so. A great lawyer will sometimes be the one encouraging a client to settle, even in instances where the client really and truly does not want to settle.

You probably know that a bad family lawyer is not experienced in the area of family law. A bad family lawyer is not well-prepared or is so busy that he or she cannot adequately devote time to your issues. A bad family lawyer does not have a thorough grasp of the facts or of the law and, consequently, is not able to develop a cogent theory about how to settle or how to fight your case. But did you know that a bad family lawyer is also often overly confrontational, as if playing a role seen on television? This approach sometimes plays well with an uninformed client who doesn't know better. After all, "If my lawyer is being aggressive, he must be fighting for me," right? Wrong. The overly confrontational lawyer is often the kerosene added to an already burning fire. This type of lawyer is rarely, if ever, helpful in bringing the parties to an efficient resolution. It should not come as a surprise that the overly confrontational lawyer often invoices much larger fees than a competent lawyer would. Buyer beware! A bad family lawyer often simply tells you what you want to hear. These types of lawyers often sell their services based on what they will "get" you, whether it be, say, 85 per cent of the assets or 100 per cent time with the kids. These are often empty promises made to emotionally needy clients. A good lawyer will give you realistic expectations regarding your legal entitlements, not just tell you what you want to hear.

LESSON 4

Understand Your Legal Entitlements from the Very Beginning of Your Case

What Are You Entitled To?

At the start of a family law dispute, most people have little actual knowledge of their legal entitlements. The initial role of your lawyer in such a situation is to advise you of the range of outcomes you can expect. This is the basis from which everything else will flow. Once you understand what to expect, you can make a decision about what is a fair resolution. Once you have a concept of what a fair resolution looks like, your prospects of achieving a sensible compromise increase and negotiations can move towards achieving an outcome close to that fair resolution.

Taking Advice from Your Former Partner and from Friends

Often, the first thing clients say to us is, "My ex said that I won't receive any more than ...." It may sound obvious, but your ex is generally not worried about protecting your interests and will say to you whatever he or she believes will put pressure on you to view the negotiation more favourably for him or her. Do not take advice from your former partner when it comes to working out what is fair or what your legal entitlements are. An extension of that position is that you should not take legal advice from your friends. Your friends, who love you and care about you, are emotionally invested in your dispute. While they may represent a great support structure for you, they are often the purveyors of bad legal advice. Beware of the friend's cousin's roommate's sister whose lawyer got him or her 100 per cent of everything. The odds are that whatever case is being referred to is factually very different from yours and, often, some of the facts from the original story have been miscommunicated. Once you have selected your great lawyer, you should rely on him or her alone for legal advice.

LESSON 5

Take Simple Steps to Minimise
Your Own Legal Costs

How to Make Things Easier for Your Lawyer—and Control Your Legal Costs in the Process

Lawyers cost money. Lawyers can cost a lot of money depending on the case. Most lawyers calculate their fee based on the time they spend working for you. A lawyer may charge between $300 and $600 per hour, depending on his or her location, quality, and experience. For a lawyer, time truly equals money. There are many ways that you can control your legal costs. You can prepare a detailed written history and chronology of your case before you see your lawyer. This will save you time at the initial conference with your lawyer, as then you will not have to remember, recite, or rehash your life's story. The lawyer will already have it, and will be able to spend more time offering his or her advice rather than on learning the background. In addition, sometimes people are nervous when first speaking to a lawyer. Writing down a chronological history ahead of time allows you to put more detail into it and to proceed at your own pace. You can compile any documents you are requested to produce, and then present these to your lawyer promptly and in an organised format. Just think of the time difference for your lawyer if you present him or her with a garbage bag full of financial documents in no particular order as opposed to presenting him or her with all of your financial documents organised in a folder with tabs for guidance. If you save your lawyer time, you are saving yourself money. You should organise or conduct any necessary investigations as quickly, and as early in the process, as possible.

If your case is based upon a particular theory, for instance, that your former partner claims to be unemployed but, in fact, is working for cash, then you may need to perform investigations to prove that your former partner is receiving cash under the table. You should undertake those investigations at the start of the process. This way, you do not run your case for weeks or months only to find later that you can't prove your suspicions. It is better to obtain the information at the outset and to let the result of the investigation direct your path. In this way, you can put forward a realistic settlement proposal.

Generally, you do not get everything you want in a court case. If you settle, you get some of what you want. If the dispute is decided by a judge, you may get none of what you want. It is better to seek a realistic settlement and to retain some control over the outcome of the dispute, as opposed to letting a judge decide. You should be open to negotiations continuously. This means that an agreement can be reached at any time during the process. You should make genuine offers based on the law and the facts, without submitting an offer that is merely posturing.

You may desperately want your lawyer to convey, in the letters he or she prepares on your behalf, the pain that you are feeling arising from your former partner's approach. Rarely does this accomplish anything other than to prompt a similarly emotional letter in return. A simple rule of thumb in these situations is, if it feels good, you probably shouldn't do it. You should comply with court directions. If a court considers that you are not following its orders, or that you are running an argument that is frivolous, it can (and will) impose an order on you to force you to pay your former partner's legal costs. This means that you will have to pay the costs incurred by your former partner to enforce an order you breached or to respond to your frivolous argument. Costs orders hurt!

You should make an early offer. Doing so can display your good faith, thereby enhancing the prospects of a negotiated settlement, and can minimise the risk of wasting time and money through court action. You should compromise your position and settle. At some point, the decision about whether or not to settle has to include a consideration of the costs of not settling. Settling can be the more commercially reasonable path.

When dealing with your lawyer, time equals money, so do the following things:

- Get to the point. Have a game plan specifying what you want to talk about and the questions you need answers to. (Write out a list of your questions in advance to act as a reminder.)
- Use email to condense information and questions you may have, as phone calls (especially for those whose conversations stray) can be long and meandering. Emails are a great way to set out multiple ideas and questions and to receive specific replies. Emails are an efficient way to communicate.
- Refrain from emoting, as lawyers are more expensive and less qualified than your therapist when dealing with your emotional well-being.
- Listen to your lawyer's advice. You are free to reject the advice, but doing so may lead to additional or unnecessary legal expenses.

How Long Will This Process Take?

The initial response to this question is, "It will take as long as you and your former partner want it to take." If you are both able to reach a settlement agreement early in the process, the time taken to implement that agreement will be very short. If you are unable to reach a compromise agreement and want a judge to make the decision for you, the process will be lengthy and expensive. If you and your former partner have negotiated a complete agreement and you go to a lawyer simply to document the agreement, then your agreement can be finalised in about four weeks. If there is a dispute that must proceed to a court hearing, the current delays in the court system are such that the entire process could take up to three years.

Property

Preparation

Before you can commence serious negotiations to resolve how the property will be divided, you will need to provide your solicitor with a statement setting out your current assets, liabilities, superannuation fund, income, and expenses using a form supplied by the court (your solicitor can provide you with that blank form); copies of documents evidencing your current financial position, including bank statements, tax returns, superannuation fund statements, appraisals of real estate value, and payslips; and a summary of the financial history of your relationship detailing the sources of funds during that period and the roles you each played. This material then forms the basis for any proposal you submit to your former partner, and for any disclosure material you have to provide to him or her.

What Is the Formula for Dividing Property?

When deciding how to divide property, there is no formula, but the law does follow a basic, three-stage process. The first stage is to identify and assign value to all the assets and liabilities of the parties, whether those assets are in one party's name, in both parties' names jointly, or in the name of a company or a trust. In this step, the total value of the net assets of the parties is calculated, including any superannuation fund, which is to be divided.

The second stage is to analyse the historical contributions to this asset pool by each party. This step assesses the contributions of each party over the history of the relationship (including salary, parenting, maintaining the house, inheritances, gifts from relatives) and then, based on those relative contributions, calculates each party's entitlement as a percentage of the net asset pool. For example, at the end of this stage, one party may be entitled to 60 per cent of the assets and the other party to 40 per cent.

The third stage is to analyse the differing future needs of each party. This step considers each party's future needs based on such things as income earning capacity, age, health status, and the need to care for children, and can result in the disadvantaged party receiving an increased percentage share of the asset pool. As an example, at the end of this process the party who received a 50 per cent share of the assets based on contributions may receive an extra 10 per cent, for a total share of 60 per cent of the entire asset pool.

Your lawyer will walk you through this three-stage process, as it applies to the facts of your particular situation, and at the conclusion of that process, will provide you with an estimate of the likely share of the total net assets to which you are entitled.

Proposing a Resolution

Once you understand your likely entitlement, you can enter into meaningful negotiations with your former partner. These negotiations may present you with various options for achieving an acceptable outcome for your consideration, including which assets have to be sold, whether you can afford to retain a particular asset or debt, whether you need to divide a superannuation account, and whether you want to trade off a superannuation entitlement against a more liquid asset. You can finalise an acceptable compromise agreement by lodging consent orders with the court.

LESSON 6

Be Practical, Conciliatory, and Child-Focussed When Developing a Parenting Plan with Your Former Partner

Parenting

Dispute Resolution Counselling

<u>What Is It?</u>

At the risk of stating the obvious, it is universally accepted that the best people to resolve disputes over parenting issues are the parents themselves. The family law system recognises this principle by requiring separated parents who have a dispute over parenting to meet with a counsellor in an attempt to achieve an assisted resolution to that dispute before they can take any legal action. This is compulsory mediation. Counselling services have been set up through the court system and by the federal government to help people resolve their parenting disputes. These counsellors, who are called family dispute resolution practitioners (FDRP), are experienced in, and effective at, mediating disputes relating to children. You can start the process by contacting a dispute resolution service, such as that operated by Interrelate (<u>interrelate.org. au</u>), to arrange a meeting with an FDRP. The purpose for your initial meeting would be to establish a timetable for the counselling process. The FDRP would typically notify the other parent in writing about the process and invite his or her involvement.

The costs of counselling depend on the provider. The government subsidises some family dispute resolution (FDR) services. The Family Relationships Centre, and other FDR services funded by the Australian government, usually charge a nominal fee and may apply a sliding scale depending on your income. Private FDR services are more expensive and will charge an hourly rate. FDR services funded by the Australian government, such as those provided by the Family Relationships Centre, generally take longer, as there are often large waiting lists. It is not uncommon to wait three months before you obtain a first appointment with a government-subsidised FDR service. For this reason, it is usually a good idea to book in to these services as soon as possible after you separate. Private FDR is more expensive but does not involve delays. Private FDR allows you to shop around for the first available, which is critical if there is some urgency in your dispute.

What if Your Former Partner Won't Attend Counselling?

It always takes two to tango. Once you engage a counsellor, that counsellor will usually approach your former partner to arrange for his or her attendance at a counselling session. If your former partner refuses to be involved in any counselling, you will then be faced with the choice of doing nothing or commencing court proceedings. Your counsellor can issue a certificate to confirm counselling is not possible, and this certificate will entitle you to commence court proceedings. Once the dispute proceeds to court, the judge, when considering the matter, will take into account your former partner's refusal to attend counselling. The refusal may damage your former partner's case.

What Is the Formula for Working Out Where the Children Live?

There is no formula applied by a court to work out where your children will live. The primary rule is that the best interests of the child are the paramount consideration. The starting point is always that you and your former partner are in the best position to come up with a parenting plan specifying the children's living arrangements. When it comes to the needs of children, parents know best. There are many factors that are taken into account in considering this issue, including the historical relationship of each parent with the child, and the nature of their respective roles in the child's day-to-day life; the age of the children and the ages of their parents; the mental and physical health of the children and of their parents; the relationship of the children to each other; where each parent will be living after separation; the capacity of each parent to look after the emotional and financial needs of the children; the location of extended family and the family support network; the location of friends of the parents and of the child, and the nature of that extended support network; and depending on the maturity of the children, the children's wishes. By coming up with a solution for themselves, parents can take into account all relevant issues, including their individual work commitments (such as shift work rosters), the availability of childminding (including day care and grandparents), and the children's social and extracurricular commitments (such as sports, dance classes, and sleepovers). An arrangement set up by the parents will be much cleverer than an arrangement imposed by a judge.

Will the Children's Own Views Be Considered?

Whether the views of a child are considered important or not depends on the age and maturity of the child. It is relatively clear that if the child is seventeen and doesn't want to live with one parent, a court order to force the child to live with that parent is of little value. Similarly, few people would argue that the wishes of a two-year-old should determine where that child lives. Usually, a child's wishes are considered relevant beginning when the child is around thirteen years of age. There is no hard and fast rule as to the exact age when a child's opinion becomes important, as the relevance of that opinion will depend on such factors as the emotional maturity of the child, the capacity of the child to effectively express his or her views, the history of the child's engagement with one or both parents, and the influence of either parent over the child's ability to formulate his or her views. Generally, the older the child, the more likely it is that his or her wishes will play an important part in the decision as to where the child should live or how much time the child will spend with each parent.

Can You Move House with the Children?

After separating, the parents are often faced with decisions about where they, and the children in their care, should live. Many factors can impact this decision, including the children's relationships with their friends; the children's schooling arrangements; the job opportunities available to the primary carer; the children's day-care or after-school-care needs; and the availability of support from extended family and friends. The basic principle is that the parent who is responsible for the primary care of the children can relocate with the children when he or she has a good reason for the move and the move is in the best interests of the children. It is always advisable for a parent making a move, no matter how geographically small that move may be, to provide full details of the move to the other parent and to obtain the other parent's consent to that move in advance. Apart from anything else, both parents are entitled to know where the children are living and in what conditions. If you relocate without consent, you may find that the other parent obtains a court order requiring you to return with the children, as the family court does not look favourably upon a parent who unilaterally reduces the amount of time that the other parent can spend with the children by moving.

If the children live primarily with you, then how far you can move away with the children without the permission of the other parent depends upon the impact of the move on the ability of the other parent to maintain a meaningful relationship with the children. The difficulty with any relocation is that it may prevent the children from continuing, or limit their ability to continue, to have a meaningful relationship with the parent who is left behind. As a general rule, if you have primary care of the children and want to move house with them, and if that the move results in your having to change their school or forces changes to the time the children can spend with the other parent, then you should seek the other parent's agreement to that arrangement. That agreement can take into account such matters as who is to pay for the costs of travelling; how the time that the non-primary carer spends with the child can be rearranged to minimise the impact of travelling on the quality of the time spent together; and whether it is appropriate to consider giving the non-primary carer some additional time with the children in view of any disruption to his or her time with the children caused by the move.

If the proposed move by the primary carer will result in a reduction in the other parent's time with the children, and if the other parent objects, then the primary carer will have to present compelling reasons to justify the move. The move may be required because the primary carer needs to move closer to a strong family support network; needs to move to take up a new job offer; or needs to move to be able to live with a new life partner. Importantly, the benefits to the children of these factors would have to outweigh the reduced time they would have to spend with the other parent. Balancing these matters can often be a difficult exercise, so if you are considering relocating with the children, never take any action without first consulting a lawyer to carefully analyse the reasons for the move, the benefits that will accrue to the children, and the means by which you can minimise the negative impacts on the children.

> **Example:** Cameron and Tracy, who are separated, both live in Sydney. Tracy is the primary carer of their nine-year-old child, Sue, who spends four nights per fortnight with Cameron. Cameron is unemployed. Tracy is offered an amazing job in Brisbane at a salary five times anything she could earn in Sydney. As a result, she wants to move to Brisbane with Sue. Tracy argues that the move is in Sue's best interests because the new job will represent financial security for Sue; Tracy's family lives in Brisbane and can help her with supervision of Sue; and Tracy can facilitate contact between Cameron and Sue by (a) paying for return flights for Cameron to come to Brisbane twice per year for a week each time, (b) paying for return flights for Sue to go to Sydney four times per year for a week each time, (c) paying for the installation of a high-speed Internet connection at Cameron's house and in Tracy's own house, with Skype and FaceTime, to facilitate daily communication, and (d) acquiring various apps to facilitate communication between Cameron and Tracy about Sue's progress. Cameron objects to the proposed move because his overnight time with Sue would reduce from 104 nights per year to about 40 nights per year, and this would negatively impact his relationship with

Sue. He is also concerned about the disruption to Sue's schooling and the loss of her school friendships.

Given that Cameron is unemployed, that Sue's financial security is an issue, and that Tracy has proposed a comprehensive arrangement for Sue to spend time with Cameron, Tracy's application is approved by the court.

What Child Support Will Have to Be Paid?

Child support is the amount of money that one parent has to pay to the other for the costs of maintaining the children. The calculation of that amount is based on a formula set out in the legislation, which takes into account the taxable incomes of both parties, the parties' need to support themselves and other dependents, the age of the children, and the number of nights each week that the children spend with each parent. You can calculate the amount of child support that is likely to be payable by inputting the relevant data into the Child Support Estimator on the website of the Department of Human Services at https://processing.csa. gov.au/estimator/Parents.aspx.

As soon as you are separated, either you or your former partner can apply for child support by lodging an application with the Department of Human Services. The Department will process the application and arrange to collect the child support for you.

Is "Equal Time" Shared Parenting the Starting Point?

The short answer to this question is no. Although the court generally has to consider equal-time shared parenting as an option, there is no presumption under the family law that it is in child's best interests to spend equal time with each parent. Indeed, most parenting arrangements structured through the family court do not involve equal time with each parent. The reason for this is a very practical one. It is not common for both parents to have available the time and the flexibility for each to be able to manage the children for 50 per cent of the time.

When Will Equal-Time Parenting Work?

Generally, for equal-time shared parenting to work effectively, the two parents must have strong communication skills and be focussed on the welfare of the children. While that may sound like an obvious statement, the fact is that it is surprisingly difficult for many parents, post-separation, to effectively communicate with their former partner about the children, given the emotion surrounding the breakdown of their relationship. Successful parenting in any household before separation demands a great deal of co-operation and teamwork between the two parents. After a separation, when there are effectively two households, if the children are to spend 50 per cent of their time with each parent, the degree of co-operation required between the parents is even greater. Excellent communication skills are essential to ensure that the two households operate seamlessly from the perspective of the children. For the children, ideally, the two households should seem as one. If parents are not good communicators, a court will generally not consider an equal-time shared parenting arrangement to be appropriate. The key requirements for the success of an equal-time parenting plan are that the two parents abandon their own personal differences, focus on meeting the children's needs, and have an ability to communicate with each other effectively, and civilly, about those needs. Another key element to successful equal-time parenting is that the two parents do not live far apart. The closer they are, the more readily they can both contribute to the children's schooling requirements, and the less travel the children have to undertake to or from the parents' homes and to or from school. For equal-time parenting to work, you will need to manage the risk of disruption, disorganisation, and stress to children whose lives may be overloaded with school and extracurricular activities, and the problem of travel if you and the other parent are not geographically very close.

What Is Your Parenting Plan?

Good parenting arrangements in separated families do not just happen. They must be carefully planned, managed, and maintained—and this requires the parents to communicate well. In order to resolve the parenting arrangements for your family, whether by agreement with your former partner or through the court system, the first thing you should do is to prepare a detailed parenting plan. This plan can detail how the parents propose to resolve disputes that may arise over the children. It can set out how the parents will communicate with each other, whether in person, by text, by using a communication book, or by email. It can ensure that the time the child spends with each parent includes weekends, holidays, and normal weekdays; allows each parent to be involved in the child's daily routine, and occasions and events that are of particular significance to the child; and allows the child to be involved in occasions and events that are of special significance to each parent. The plan can analyse each party's work commitments (and each parent's consequent availability), the changeover arrangements, the financial arrangements for the children, emergency arrangements (e.g. for when a child is sick), and the parents' joint approach to discipline. You may find it helpful to use a parenting plan template to guide you through the planning process. A good guide is located at http://www.familyrelationships.gov.au/BrochuresandPublications/Pages/parentingplanguide.aspx.

Reality-Testing Your Parenting Plan

Before presenting your plan to your former partner, you should review it with another person to test whether your proposal is realistic. You should consider how you will supervise the children when they are with you if you are working full time. Analyse how flexible your employer would be if you needed to spend time with the children on account of an emergency or on school holidays. Look at the travelling times involved with changeovers and how many changeovers you are proposing each week to see if these are sensible. Check how your plan will fit in with your former partner's work and other commitments. Consider whether your plan effectively takes into account the children's ages, their extracurricular activities, and depending on their level of maturity, their individual wishes.

To minimise the risk of facing unexpected hurdles that prevent your former partner from agreeing to your plan, you can check the various elements of the plan with key players. You could discuss with your employer whether your own employment arrangement carries with it the flexibility you need to deal with children's illnesses or school holidays. You could discuss with your extended family whether the support you need from them will be consistently available. You could discuss with the children's day care facility or school how they can support you in implementing the plan. You could discuss with a counsellor or a lawyer to see whether they feel there are any weaknesses in the plan before you put it to your former partner. Once you have completed the reality test, and reworked the plan to take into account any issues arising from that process, you can be confident that the plan you are proposing is practical and achievable.

Proposing a Positive Resolution—Constructive Offers

Given the tension that can exist following separation, it is sometimes difficult to approach parenting issues in a creative fashion and with an appreciation of the position of your former partner. But, in fact, this is what successful parenting requires you to do. Parenting is a "team sport," and unless you and your former partner are able to focus on the children's best interests and can work together to foster those interests, your parenting arrangements will be riddled with conflict and will damage the children. With that in mind, negotiations for parenting arrangements should be approached positively, flexibly, and with a view to constructive compromises. If either parent draws a line in the sand that limits his or her flexibility, then a successful parenting plan is an unlikely outcome. In order to offer a constructive proposal, you should carefully consider the needs of the children and those of your former partner. You should use positive language both when writing the proposal and when discussing it with your former partner. You should listen carefully to the matters put to you by your former partner and, if they are mature, your children. You should not commence a parenting negotiation with an ambit claim. The common technique in negotiations of asking for much more than you realistically hope ever to achieve will often be counterproductive, because it can indicate an unwillingness to approach the issue with the children's best interests in mind. Do not be combative, for example, by simply dismissing the issues raised by your former partner as unreasonable or impractical. Work through his or her proposals carefully to explain why they won't work. Put forth a proposal that is practically achievable, that takes into account issues that your former partner has raised, and that represents compromises you are willing to make. Your former partner's approach to the negotiation, whether constructive or not, is something over which you have no control. By being constructive in your approach, you are sending a message that you are prepared to be reasonable and responsible, and you thereby increase your chances of achieving a sensible resolution without the need for court involvement. Following this advice will maximise the prospects of your achieving, and successfully implementing, an effective parenting plan.

CHAPTER 3

NEGOTIATING SOLUTIONS

Chapter Summary

In this chapter we provide you with alternatives for solutions to finalise your property and parenting disputes without having to resort to the courts. We show you the key elements needed to maximise the prospects of a successful negotiation. The lessons to be discussed in this chapter are as follows:

Lesson 1—Carefully Choose the Right Lawyer to Assist You with Your Family Law Dispute

Lesson 2—A Willingness to Compromise by Both Parties Is Essential to Resolving Your Dispute by Negotiation

Lesson 3—In Order to Maximise the Prospects of Successfully Resolving Your Family Law Dispute, You Must Be Very Well-Prepared for the Negotiation Process

Lesson 4—Speak to Your Lawyer to Find Out What Alternatives Are Available for Resolving Your Dispute

How Can You Maximise the Prospects of a Successful Negotiation?

Negotiating an outcome to your property and/or parenting dispute can be one of the best ways to resolve your family law issues after separation. There are three main reasons for this. Firstly, when comparing the money you might spend negotiating a resolution to the costs of a contested battle through a court, it is clear that a negotiated resolution is always a more cost-effective way to proceed. Secondly, you would be hard-pressed to find a person who has uttered the sentences, "I really enjoyed that family court experience. I loved being cross-examined on my life and marriage, and I look forward to co-parenting with my former partner in the future!" The court process can be expensive, emotionally draining, and time-consuming. In comparison, negotiating a resolution is a more amicable way of resolving family issues. An amicable resolution promotes the prospects of a better relationship between you and your former partner in the future, which is particularly important when there are children to consider. Thirdly, negotiation provides you and your former partner with greater control over the process and the final outcomes. We have detailed below a number of ways you can increase the likelihood of a successful negotiation process.

LESSON 1

Carefully Choose the Right Lawyer to Assist You with Your Family Law Dispute

Choose a Good Lawyer

In chapter 2, we discussed the differences between a great lawyer and a bad lawyer. Revisit that chapter now, as you will need a great lawyer to help you with this process. Having a great lawyer on your team will ensure that you optimise your prospects of a successful negotiation. It is important that you obtain advice about your entitlements early on. If you have just separated, you will likely have very little knowledge of your legal entitlements. This may be the first time you are going through a separation or divorce. While you may have a family member or friend who has gone through the process, each person's experience and fact situation is different. Getting advice from a lawyer at the beginning will assist you in understanding how family law works and how entitlements are considered.

A family separation is not something that one expects to have to deal with when he or she first enters a relationship. For this reason, you might not know where to find a good lawyer. Here are some tips to finding a good lawyer. Speak to relatives, colleagues, and friends who have gone through a similar process and find out about their experiences with their lawyers. Don't go by recommendations alone. Meet with a lawyer and see if you have a good rapport. Contact your local Law Society to obtain a list of family law specialists in your area. Check the experience of the lawyer you are planning to meet with by either asking the lawyer about his or her experience and background or checking the lawyer's website or Internet profile. In this way you can find out what kind of disputes the lawyer focusses on and discover whether he or she has written any articles or blog entries on topics that relate to your particular family law situation.

LESSON 2

A Willingness to Compromise by Both Parties Is Essential to Resolving Your Dispute by Negotiation

Have a Willingness to Compromise

A great lawyer can only take you part of the way towards a negotiated solution. It takes two people to negotiate effectively, and if one person is compromising while the other is stubbornly maintaining his or her initial position, the chances of resolving the dispute by negotiation will be slim. In most cases, each party to a family law dispute will obtain legal advice about their entitlements. That advice will depend on the facts that were given to the lawyer by his or her client. It is not uncommon for there to be disagreement about the facts of the relationship. Let's face it, if there were agreement, the former couple could probably sort it out without lawyers. It is not uncommon for the parties' initial negotiating positions to be poles apart, but a willingness to compromise is essential if both are to move towards a resolution. Those who start negotiations at one point and do not move from that position at all will find that the negotiation process stops there. There is nowhere to go with negotiations if one party will not compromise on his or her position.

This is when having a good lawyer is important. A good lawyer will provide you with a range of possible outcomes and give you guidance throughout the negotiations. Sometimes you will be willing to compromise your position but your former partner will not. A good lawyer will advise you about when to stop negotiating and to commence court proceedings. There is little point persisting with negotiations if the other party is stubbornly holding on to an unreasonable position. Persisting in such a case will only cost you time and money.

Adopt a Respectful Approach to Negotiation

Negotiation has a lot to do with attitudes. Have you ever heard of the saying "you can catch more flies with honey than with vinegar"? It is generally easier to persuade others with polite requests and a positive attitude, rather than with demands and negativity. When negotiating, there are some basic things to consider, as we have set out below.

Use Positive Language

At the point of separation, and immediately after it, your relationship with your former partner is likely to be at its lowest point. You are both likely to be at some stage of the grieving process, feeling emotions such as guilt, relief, sadness, anger, betrayal, and loneliness. The exact emotions that each of you feel will depend upon who instigated the separation, the circumstances of the separation, and the stage of grief that you are currently experiencing. All of these factors suggest that at this point in time, communication will be difficult. And yet, for negotiations to progress, this is the very time when good communication skills are essential. While it may be tempting to make demands and threats, and to criticise conduct, very rarely will this get you what you want. In fact, it is more likely to cause a further rift between you and your former partner.

Positive language and reasoned arguments are the tools you need to use to get your point of view across to convince your former partner, or his or her lawyer, of your position. Putting forward a well-considered argument supported by the law is much more persuasive than shouting demands. Given that emotions will be running high, it is very easy to further alienate your former partner by choosing the wrong language. We have experienced clients' shock, anger, and hurt when they have received a letter from the solicitor representing their former partner that minimises their role as a parent or as a homemaker, or understates the financial contributions they made. To effectively negotiate, it is important to acknowledge the positive things that your former partner contributed to the relationship, both financial and non-financial.

LESSON 3

In Order to Maximise the Prospects of Successfully Resolving Your Family Law Dispute, You Must Be Very Well-Prepared for the Negotiation Process

Understand the Approach of Your Former Partner, and That of His or Her Lawyer, to Negotiations

There are many different styles of negotiation. If you are able to explain to your lawyer your former partner's personality, or the matters he or she regards as important, then your lawyer will be better positioned to structure negotiations in a fashion that enhances the prospect of reaching agreement. The same is true if your solicitor knows your former partner's solicitor and his or her historical approach to negotiations.

> **Example:** Blake and Rosanna are having negotiations to finalise their financial affairs after their separation. Blake is fifty-nine and will soon have access to his superannuation fund. Rosanna is forty-seven with a lengthy working life ahead. Rosanna knows that Blake wants to retain his superannuation fund because it will soon provide him with access to a very good pension. Rosanna's solicitor uses this knowledge to negotiate a better deal for Rosanna, as the solicitor knows that Blake will pay Rosanna a premium to keep his superannuation fund.

Alternatively, you may know that your former partner has a controlling personality and feels that he or she must "win." Your lawyer may then be able to structure negotiations in a manner that ensures your former partner can identify the outcome he or she achieves as a win.

Property

Disclosure

Family law requires that parties provide full and frank disclosure in all property disputes. This means that you and your former partner are required to give each other all of the financial documentation and information that explains your financial position. To maximise the prospect of an early successful negotiation, you need to comply fully with this disclosure obligation at the earliest opportunity.

The first step in any property dispute is to gather your financial material. Your lawyer will provide you with a list of all the material required. As a starting point, you should gather the following things:

- bank statements for all bank accounts that are in your name solely, or jointly with another person (including mortgages, credit cards, and savings accounts);
- your tax returns for the last three financial years;
- current statements for all of your superannuation accounts;
- the most recent statement if you have a bank account with someone else (e.g., a parent, a sibling, or a new partner);
- documents relevant to any business or company operated by you or your partner;
- documents that confirm the current value of any asset and/or any liability held by either you or your partner.

Valuations

If you anticipate there will be a disagreement over the valuation of a house, a superannuation fund, a business, or some other asset, you can reduce the risk of that being an impediment to negotiations by obtaining either a formal or an informal valuation/appraisal of that asset at an early stage. By obtaining two or three market appraisals from local real estate agents explaining the house value, or by obtaining a letter from your accountant explaining the rationale behind his or her assessment of the value of the business, you possibly eliminate "the unknown factor," which sometimes prevents a settlement from being reached.

Parenting

A Clear Parenting Plan

When you meet with your former partner to negotiate arrangements for parenting, you should have formulated a detailed plan that spells out the practicalities of your proposal. Many negotiations fail because one party formulates a proposal that is shown to be impractical, and is then unable to move away from that position. A clear parenting plan will identify, at a detailed level, arrangements for communication, changeovers, supervision, weekends and school holidays, and special days (e.g., birthdays, Father's Day, and Mother's Day, Christmas, and Easter). Before bringing your proposal to a negotiation, you should road-test it with a friend or relative to ensure that it works. For example, there is no point in having the children for half of every school holiday period when you are in full-time employment and do not have any ability to take time off work to supervise them during every school holiday period.

Understanding and Acknowledging the Qualities of Both Parents

A clever way to successfully negotiate is to acknowledge your former partner's strengths as a parent. This will diffuse tension and create a positive atmosphere for negotiations. The reverse is also true. If you are critical of your former partner's parenting history (e.g., "You never attended a parent–teacher evening"), then the prospects of negotiating a successful resolution are reduced. While you may feel better criticising your former partner's parenting limitations, those criticisms rarely have anything to do with the parenting issues in dispute.

Identifying Risk Factors for Children

Violence/abuse or alienation/attachment are crucial issues when it comes to parenting disputes. These issues must be identified early, because when they exist, they may indicate that negotiation is not appropriate or that a form of specialised mediation should be considered.

LESSON 4

Speak to Your Lawyer to Find Out What Alternatives Are Available for Resolving Your Dispute

What Are Your Negotiation Options?

Sorting It Out Yourselves

Where former partners are good communicators who have been able to separate without conflict, there is a strong possibility that they will have the ability to sit down around the kitchen table to formulate a basic agreement between themselves. We always suggest that before that meeting occurs, each party should obtain legal advice to explain their entitlements under family law. This way, when they have their discussion, they will understand their basic rights. If you can reach an agreement this way, your lawyers will merely have to process the agreement through the court system to make it binding.

Mediation

Mediation is a form of negotiation that involves a mediator acting as an assistant to aid the parties in reaching an agreement. The mediator has experience in the role and helps the parties to understand their needs, communicate their views, and compromise their position. The mediator's role changes depending upon the type of mediation the parties choose. A mediator can act as a facilitator whose only role is to structure the process to assist the parties in reaching a settlement. This type of mediator does not make recommendations or give advice according to his or her own opinion to the parties. A facilitative mediation focusses on the needs and interests of the parties. Alternatively, a mediator can act as an evaluator who assists the parties in reaching an agreement by highlighting the weaknesses of their position, predicting how a judge would view a certain issue, and making recommendations based on his or her own experience. An evaluative mediation focusses on the legal rights of the parties and the legal concept of fairness.

With or without Lawyers?

The parties can attend a mediation without their lawyers. Doing this can sometimes create a less formal environment, which can help put both parties at ease. It is quite easy to arrange this type of mediation by contacting a mediator directly to set up a meeting. Even if you are thinking of attending a mediation without lawyers, it is a good idea to meet with your lawyer beforehand to take advice and gain a thorough understanding of your own legal position. By being well-prepared, you increase the chances of a successful mediation and become disabused of unreasonable expectations you may otherwise hold. The process may involve two or more meetings with the mediator to ensure that by the time you and your former partner actually meet for the mediation itself, you understand the process, you are well-prepared, and time is not wasted dealing with administrative or irrelevant matters. You and your former partner can also arrange a mediation and bring your own lawyers with you to the mediation session. The lawyers actively participate in the mediation session and give advice to their clients. This form of mediation can be very effective when one or both parties feel uncomfortable with the process and lack confidence in their own ability to deal with issues that arise in a mediation.

How Do You Choose a Mediator?

The mediator you choose, and the type of mediation you use, will depend on the personalities and preferences of you and your former partner. You should discuss with your lawyer the type of mediation that, and the particular mediator who, would suit your situation. If your lawyer is experienced, he or she will have dealt with a number of mediators and have a clear view on the right one for you. Alternatively, you could contact a private mediation service and ask them to supply you with a mediator. Locating a private mediation service is as easy as

Googling "private mediation." You should ensure that the mediator you choose has experience in resolving family disputes.

Negotiations between Your Lawyers

<u>Settlement Meetings</u>

We have resolved many disputes by arranging informal round-table meetings between the parties and their lawyers. These meetings will usually take place in the office of one of the lawyers and will last between two and eight hours, depending on the complexity of the issues. The parties can structure the meeting as they wish. They can all meet in the one room together, or they can remain in separate rooms with only the lawyers meeting to negotiate. We have a very high success rate with these meetings resolving all issues.

<u>Collaborative Law</u>

Collaborative law is a concept developed in the USA that is proving highly successful in Australia. The parties and their lawyers work together (sometimes with the assistance of third parties such as counsellors, accountants, and/or financial planners) to attempt to resolve the dispute. One of the key elements of this process is a commitment by the parties and the lawyers to do their best to resolve the dispute, coupled with an agreement by the parties not to proceed to court while negotiations are progressing. If the dispute is not resolved and the parties wish to take it to court, then both lawyers are disqualified from representing the parties in court and both parties must retain new lawyers. The concept is designed to provide incentives to the parties and their lawyers to resolve the dispute collaboratively.

Arbitration

Binding arbitration is available to parties involved in a family law financial dispute. Arbitration is an alternative to court, and the parties can take up this option by agreement. The arbitrator acts like a judge to decide the outcome of the dispute. An arbitration will normally follow the court process, but it is much less formal. The parties can appoint an arbitrator and can then submit the details of their respective claims to the arbitrator in person at an arbitration hearing or simply in writing. The arbitrator is very experienced in both family law and arbitration. Following the hearing, the arbitrator will make a decision that will bind all parties. One of the major advantages of arbitration is that the parties can achieve a formal decision for their dispute far more quickly than through the family court (as quickly as three months, compared to two years through court). In addition, the total cost of the arbitration will be far less than the total cost of a court hearing. The final key advantage of arbitration is that, following recent amendments to the law, the result is binding, with each party having only limited rights to have the decision reviewed by an appeal.

CHAPTER 4

FINALISING YOUR PROPERTY AGREEMENT

Chapter Summary

In this chapter, we aim to guide you through the process of finalising your property agreement with your partner to ensure that you have a deal that cannot subsequently be changed. The lessons to be discussed in this chapter are as follows:

Lesson 1—Don't Rely on a Handshake Deal or a Promise from Your Former Partner. Make Sure You Formalise Your Deal with Court Consent Orders or a Binding Financial Agreement

Lesson 2—Tell Your Lawyer about Every Aspect of Your Agreement, and Make Sure Everything That You and Your Former Partner Have Agreed to Is Included in the Written Agreement

Lesson 3—As Soon as You Reach an Agreement, Reduce the Risk of Losing It by Moving Quickly to Formalise It as Either Court Consent Orders or a Binding Financial Agreement

Lesson 4—Take Advantage of the Tax Relief and Stamp Duty Exemptions Available When You Settle by Way of Court Consent Orders or a Binding Financial

Agreement, as This Could Save You Tens of Thousands of Dollars

Lesson 5—Avoid Disputes When You Separate by, at the Beginning of Your Relationship, Entering into a Binding Financial Agreement Setting Out What Will Happen to Your Assets if Your Relationship Ends

LESSON 1

Don't Rely on a Handshake Deal or a Promise from Your Former Partner. Make Sure You Formalise Your Deal by Way of Court Consent Orders or a Binding Financial Agreement

Why Do You Need to Document Your Financial Agreement?

Our clients often ask us why they need to legally document their agreement with their former partner and why they can't just shake hands and have the matter finalized. There are three main reasons for finalising your agreement in a formal way. Firstly, there is the need for guaranteed finality in order to move on. Secondly, you will want to avoid the risk of outside influences affecting your deal down the track. Thirdly, there are significant tax and stamp duty benefits that come with legally formalising your agreement.

Guaranteeing Finality and Moving On

Separations are difficult, even in the best of circumstances. A key element to healing after separation is being able to move on with confidence and certainty that your new separated life is your own and that the new life you build for yourself is protected from claims by your former partner. If you finalise your settlement with your former partner with a handshake or a promise but without court orders or a binding agreement, then there is nothing to prevent your former partner from making a further claim against you months, or potentially even years, later. You must manage the risk of your former partner's trying to take a "second bite of the cherry." Even if you and your former partner write out your agreement and each sign it, it will not be a legally binding deal. The agreement will not be worth the paper it is written on.

> **Example:** Jack and Georgia, after separating, wrote out and signed an agreement that enabled Georgia to keep the house and Jack to retain his business. This

seemed very fair, because the former couple and their advisors all agreed that the house and the business were of equal value. Jack and Georgia, both happy with the agreement, didn't see lawyers. After she separated, Georgia undertook renovations to the house using money given to her by her mother. Jack's business initially did well, but two years after his separation, his biggest customer went into liquidation, which led Jack's business to shut down. Jack contacted Georgia to confirm he was broke and say that wanted a share of the house. Georgia was outraged but had to pay Jack his share of the house because under family law he retained his right to that share. Their initial agreement did not help Georgia.

The *only* way to guarantee finality is to ensure that you and your former partner formalise your agreement by obtaining either court consent orders or a binding financial agreement (for more information, see below—"What Is the Process of 'Locking In' Your Deal?").

LESSON 2

Tell Your Lawyer about Every Aspect of Your Agreement, and Make Sure Everything That You and Your Former Partner Have Agreed to Is Included in the Written Agreement

Once you reach an agreement with your former partner, it is important to include every aspect of your agreement in the court orders or binding financial agreement. Even if you have talked about something with your partner and he or she has made a promise to you, if there is no mention of that aspect of the deal in the court orders or binding financial agreement, and if your partner later changes his or her mind or reneges on that part of the deal, then you will not be able to rely on the court order or the binding financial agreement to protect your position.

> **Example:** Greg and Helen separated and then agreed to sell their house and take 50 per cent each. Helen convinced Greg to arrange, and pay $10,000, for certain essential work on the house to improve its presentation for the sale. She promised him that he would get this money back from the proceeds of the sale before doing the fifty-fifty split. Greg paid for the work out of his own money, but he didn't tell his lawyer about the arrangement because he believed Helen would do as she said. Helen's lawyer prepared the binding agreement, which confirmed that the proceeds would be divided equally, but the agreement said nothing about who would pay for the recent improvements to get the house ready for sale. Once the sale was completed, the solicitor divided the proceeds equally between Greg and Helen. When Greg asked why he hadn't received his $10,000 reimbursement, Helen denied that such was the agreement. Greg was out of pocket for the cost of the renovation work and had no claim to retrieve it.

Risk of Outside Influence

Unfortunately, when it comes to divorce and separation, everyone has an opinion about what you should do and what is a fair deal. You should assume that there are a number of outside influences affecting your former partner's decision making. For example, former partners may have family members, friends, or even a new life partner who is influencing the choices he or she makes regarding the separation and divorce. It is highly common in family law disputes for parties to reach an agreement between themselves, only for one party to be influenced by his or her new partner to change his or her mind or move the goalposts. This process can be extremely frustrating and result in increased stress and anxiety in already difficult circumstances. Outside influences will always be a factor to be dealt with in family law disputes. Everyone knows someone who has been through a separation and is ready with advice (whether the concerned party wants it or not, and whether it is relevant or not). These people can have significant influence, particularly in situations where one person has re-partnered and that new partner thus has a stake in the outcome.

> **Example:** Paul and Narelle separated and, after going through everything with their respective lawyers, reached a complete agreement detailing the division of their finances, putting it in writing. Unfortunately, before the deal could be properly documented, Paul's new partner became involved. She explained to Paul the process she went through in her own recent divorce, mentioning that her ex-husband received much more than Paul was going to receive. She convinced Paul that he was entitled to more, although she had no legal qualifications and no knowledge of the law, and even though Paul's own solicitor had advised him to proceed with the original agreed deal. Paul then reneged on the deal. The added legal costs for both parties were significant, and the eventual outcome closely reflected the original deal they had reached.

LESSON 3

As Soon as You Reach an Agreement, Reduce the Risk of Losing It by Moving Quickly to Formalise It as Either Court Consent Orders or a Binding Financial Agreement

What Is the Process of "Locking In" Your Deal?

We cannot stress enough the importance of locking in your deal in a legally binding way. Unlike with commercial deals, a family law court will not bind a person to a handshake deal. A court won't even uphold an agreement that you and your former partner may have written out together and signed. In Australia there are *only two* ways to lock in your deal: either you can use court consent orders or you can enter into a binding financial agreement.

Court Consent Orders

Court orders are a binding directive issued by a court requiring a person to do, or not to do, something. Parties *must* comply with the matters set out in the orders. If they breach an order, then they will likely find themselves brought back before the court to face enforcement proceedings or, in extreme cases, a prison sentence for contempt of court.

Court orders can be made by consent (i.e. by agreement between you and your former partner), and the process can be completed in six weeks. The process for obtaining court orders by consent is quite straightforward and relatively inexpensive. Firstly, you must reach some agreement. While going through that process, you and your former partner must make full financial disclosure to each other. There can be no secrets or withholding of information. In addition, each party must see a separate lawyer (i.e., both of you cannot go to the same lawyer). One party's lawyer will then draft an application to the court and the actual form of orders reflecting the agreement reached (e.g., sale of house, closure and dividing of bank accounts, and splitting a superannuation fund). The application to the court must set out the detailed financial information relating to the parties' assets and liabilities. Once the parties confirm that the contents of the application and the consent orders accurately reflect their agreement, they sign the documents with their solicitors and the documents are lodged with the court for approval. The court will review the documents (no one has to attend court) and, if satisfied that the arrangement is fair, will make the orders as agreed, seal the orders, and send them back to the lawyers. Once orders are sealed by the court, you can be confident that the orders are binding and your agreement is locked in.

Binding Financial Agreements

A binding financial agreement (BFA) is a written agreement between two people in a life relationship that sets out how they will divide their assets and liabilities at the end of their relationship. It is, in effect, a contract. As is the case with consent orders, each party must see a separate lawyer (both of you cannot go to the same lawyer). The BFA is prepared by one solicitor to reflect the agreement reached. The document is then submitted to the other party for approval. If both parties approve the document, they and their solicitors will sign it. Provided that the BFA meets certain basic standards, it will be binding and will prevent a court from making orders for the division of property covered by the BFA. Each party retains a copy of the signed document. The document does not have to be lodged or filed anywhere. Both parties must, however, have made full financial disclosure to each other. Again, as with consent orders, there can be no secrets or withholding of information.

A BFA can be entered into either before your relationship starts (the term *prenup* is commonly used to describe these types of agreements), during your relationship, or after the relationship is over. This process can be completed in as little as two weeks.

LESSON 4

Take Advantage of the Tax Relief and Stamp Duty Exemptions Available When You Settle by Way of Court Consent Orders or a Binding Financial Agreement, as This Could Save You Tens of Thousands of Dollars

What about Tax and Stamp Duty?

By resolving your dispute through the use of either court consent orders or a BFA, you will be able to take advantage of tax relief and stamp duty exemptions, which are available to couples upon the breakdown of their relationship. This could save you tens of thousands of dollars. Stamp duty is a very large expense charged by the state, and is normally payable when you transfer your interest in a property to another person. (For example, you and your former partner may have agreed that you would transfer your home to your former partner, who would pay you a lump sum.) Depending on the state you live in, you will be eligible to obtain a stamp duty exemption in relation to the transfer of property to or from your former partner, provided the transfer is pursuant to a court consent order or a BFA. If parties settle on a handshake deal, then the exemption will not be available to them. The stamp duty exemption is also available to parties who want to transfer property to a child or the children of either party using a BFA or court consent orders.

Capital gains tax (CGT) is a tax levied by the federal government. Normally, when you dispose of your interest in a property, you become liable to pay tax on any capital gain you make on the sale. (For example, you and your former partner may have held an investment property jointly and, as part of your agreement, that property was to be transferred into your sole name. Normally that transfer would give rise to a CGT liability.) You can obtain relief from liability for CGT in relation to property transferred pursuant to court consent orders or a BFA. The effect of CGT relief is that you don't have to pay the tax at the time the property is transferred to a former partner pursuant to court consent orders or a BFA. Instead, any accrued CGT is deferred until the person who received the property eventually disposes of it. That person alone will then have to pay that tax.

LESSON 5

Avoid Disputes When You Separate by, at the Beginning of Your Relationship, Entering into a Binding Financial Agreement Setting Out What Will Happen to Your Assets if Your Relationship Ends

Binding Financial Agreements at the Beginning of, or during, Relationships

Often people will enter into BFAs either prior to commencing their relationship or during their relationship, so that they can clearly set out what will happen to their assets and liabilities if they separate. This type of BFA is often referred to, colloquially, as a prenup. Prenup BFAs can be useful in a number of situations. An individual entering a second relationship may want to preserve his or her assets for the children from a previous relationship. A party may want to protect his or her assets where there is a significant difference in the wealth of the parties at the commencement of the relationship (e.g., the scenario of a millionaire and his mistress). Each party may want to protect inheritances that they expect to receive during their relationship. The parties can use a BFA to give special recognition to contributions made during the relationship by a high-income-earning life partner or by a life partner who has taken on the unique role of parenting a child with a disability. Where a parent, friend, or relative of one party provides a loan or gift, that party may want to have that loan or gift recognised and protected. Finally, one party may have substantial debts at the commencement of the relationship and the other party may want this "negative contribution" acknowledged so that he or she is not penalised should the relationship end.

The advantages of a prenup BFA in any of the above situations is that it promotes better communication in the long term by demonstrating that the parties have no secrets from each other. In addition, it removes sources of stress and of dispute by giving the parties certainty and control over their financial affairs. A prenup BFA will prevent either party from applying to the court at the end of the relationship to seek a division of assets different from that set out in the BFA.

CHAPTER 5

THE COURT PROCESS

Chapter Summary

If you find yourself in the situation of having to commence court proceedings, or if your former partner has commenced court proceedings, you will find in this chapter some practical guidance about the court process. The lessons to be discussed in this chapter are as follows:

Lesson 1—Don't Be Afraid of the Court Process. While Court Should Be a Last Resort, It Can Provide Solutions Where Negotiation Is Bogged Down or Not a Realistic Alternative

Lesson 2—You Should Continue Your Attempts to Negotiate a Resolution Even during the Court Process

Lesson 3—Don't Be Afraid to Use the Court Process to Help You Resolve Your Dispute in a More Efficient Manner

Lesson 4—Make Sure You Fully Understand the Potential Cost and Delay Associated with Court Proceedings Before You Venture Down That Path

When Will Court Proceedings Be Necessary?

Court proceedings become necessary for a variety of reasons. If you and your former partner cannot agree on an outcome, or if you are a long way apart in your expectations regarding a sensible outcome, then the intervention of a court may be essential. Often this position can arise when one or both parties is unreasonable or suffering a mental illness/personality disorder and refuses to compromise. Another situation making court intervention necessary is when you have made a genuine attempt to contact your former partner to attempt to resolve dispute but your former partner refused to engage in any negotiations. Continued attempts to negotiate in circumstances where it is clear that there is no commitment to the negotiation process by the other party will just increase your legal costs unnecessarily and waste your time. In circumstances where the possible outcomes are either all or nothing, you may have little choice but to commence court action. Examples of all-or-nothing cases include the following:

- One person involved in a parenting dispute wants to relocate with the children interstate or overseas.
- There are arguments over specific facts (e.g., the value of a particular asset) that neither party wants to compromise on.
- Your former partner has already started court proceedings.

LESSON 1

Don't Be Afraid of the Court Process. While Court Should Be a Last Resort, It Can Provide Solutions Where Negotiation Is Bogged Down or Not a Realistic Alternative

How Long Does the Court Process Take?

The waiting time to obtain a court decision varies depending on which Court Registry you are considering using. In Sydney, the court process to finalise a separation can take up to two years. Complex parenting disputes can remain in the court system for even longer. However, commencing court proceedings does not necessarily mean that you will become engaged in a lengthy court battle with a judge making a decision for you. Remember, the whole family court system is designed to encourage settlement between parties at every opportunity. There will be plenty of opportunities to settle your dispute along the way.

Stages of the Court Process

Before Commencing Court Action in Parenting Disputes

In most parenting disputes, before commencing court proceedings, you must try to resolve your dispute by attending compulsory mediation. The court may grant an exemption to this requirement if there is particular urgency. Compulsory mediation is undertaken by using family dispute resolution (FDR) services (see chapter 2, under "Dispute Resolution Counselling").

Before Commencing Court Action in Property Disputes

Before you can commence court action when there is a dispute over the division of property, you must disclose to your former partner all your relevant financial information.

Commencing Court Action

In Australia, either the Federal Circuit Court or the Family Court of Australia deals with family law disputes. The Family Court generally deals with more complex issues, such as parenting disputes involving serious allegations of abuse or mental health issues, and property disputes involving property with a large value and complex asset structures. If you commence court proceedings in one of these jurisdictions and that court considers that the other jurisdiction is more appropriate for your dispute, your case may be transferred to the other court, which can cause delays.

To start court proceedings, you generally need to lodge with the court an application setting out what you want, a financial statement detailing your present financial circumstances (including your assets, liabilities, income, expenses, and superannuation fund), and a short affidavit setting out the story that you intend to rely on that details the background of your claim. The other party then lodges similar documents with the court in response, setting out what he or she wants.

Interim Disputes

Once court proceedings begin, either party may want a court to make a decision on a short-term issue that needs an urgent resolution before the main dispute can continue. Such a resolution can be achieved via an interim court hearing. An interim hearing is a short hearing that takes place early in the court process, usually two to six months after an application is lodged with the court. Interim hearings relate to issues that cannot wait until the court has an opportunity to conduct a lengthy final hearing. A good example of an issue that can be dealt with at an interim hearing is a dispute regarding the place where a child should live pending the court's final decision in a parenting dispute. Another example is where parties dispute who should be entitled to live in the house while the main court case is ongoing. Interim orders might also be required when one party needs to be paid spousal maintenance so that he or she can meet his or her ordinary living expenses while the main court case is continuing. A final example is when a party needs to protect a particular asset in the period before the court makes its final decision. This may be necessary when one party threatens to sell an asset and dispose of the proceeds.

After an Application Has Been Lodged with the Court

Once the application is lodged with the court, you will be advised of a date to come to court, usually three to six months after the documents are lodged. You have to attend court on this date with your lawyer, but the process is mainly administrative in nature to assist the court in deciding how to advance the case. You do not normally have to say anything in court on this day. In matters involving a dispute over financial issues, the court may direct both parties to obtain formal valuations or produce certain documents. In parenting disputes, the court may order both parties to participate in a child dispute conference with a court counsellor. This may occur on the day you are at court or in the future, depending on the availability of the court counsellor. The appointment for this counselling session can be booked while you are at court.

Also on your first day at court, the court may appoint a future date for you and your former partner to attend a private session with a court officer for a conciliation conference (which is essentially a settlement conference wherein the court officer works together with both parties and their lawyers to try to resolve the dispute). This conference may take place three to six months after the first date in court. You must attend court for the conciliation conference with your lawyer. If you and your former partner reach agreement at a conciliation conference, you are usually able to document your agreement. The court officer can then make the court orders on the spot. This means you might leave the conciliation conference with a binding set of court orders and with your dispute finalised. If you and your former partner are unable to reach an agreement, then the court officer will usually provide both of you with a date for the final hearing before a judge. That date may be twelve to eighteen months in the future. Along the way, in the lead-up to the final court hearing date, you and your former partner may have to exchange your financial documents, obtain experts' reports (especially if there are disputes over children's arrangements or property values), exchange correspondence, and possibly make further attempts at mediation or a negotiated settlement. Sometimes the court will appoint an expert to investigate and report on issues involving children, and may order the appointment of a lawyer to represent the children (called an independent children's lawyer).

The Final Hearing

The final stage in the court process is the final hearing. In Sydney, this will usually occur between eighteen and thirty-six months after an application has been lodged. At the final hearing, both parties tell the judge their story and are questioned by the lawyer for the other party. Each party can show the judge any documents that they believe support their claim, and each party will have witnesses who can provide support to their own claims. The judge will make a decision after the final hearing.

LESSON 2

You Should Continue Your Attempts to Negotiate a Resolution Even during the Court Process

Opportunities to Resolve along the Way

Once court proceedings are commenced, you will have many opportunities to attempt to negotiate a resolution during those proceedings. Every time you and your former partner and your respective lawyers meet in court, the court officer and the lawyers will discuss the issues and attempt to reach a resolution. It is not uncommon for the commencement of court proceedings to promote a resolution of the dispute. This is because the parties are forced to focus on the realities of their dispute and because the legal costs are escalating on account of the court action. As a result, during the court process, the parties are often highly motivated to meet for their own settlement conference, with their lawyers or with a private mediator, to aid in their attempt to resolve their dispute.

LESSON 3

Don't Be Afraid to Use the Court Process to Help You Resolve Your Dispute in a More Efficient Manner

What Is a Barrister, and Do You Need One?

A barrister is a lawyer who specialises in appearing in court. Your solicitor will perform all the steps necessary to prepare your case to go to court. If your case proceeds to a court hearing, your solicitor will usually ask a barrister to represent you in the courtroom during the actual court hearing, to explain your case to the judge, to question witnesses on your behalf, and to generally protect your interests in court. Usually, you will need a barrister only if your dispute proceeds to a final court hearing.

Advantages of the Court Process

The court process forces both parties to focus on the dispute and to consider resolution. In some cases, without the commencement of court proceedings, negotiations can drag on interminably, adding unnecessarily to the expense and delay without progressing the prospects of any resolution. Disputes that are brought before the court are usually one of two types: (1) cases that cannot be resolved by the parties and that require a judge to make a decision and (2) cases where the parties need the pressure and cost of court proceedings as a motivator to help them to resolve their dispute.

LESSON 4

Make Sure You Fully Understand the Potential Cost and Delay Associated with Court Proceedings before You Venture Down That Path

Disadvantages of the Court Process

By entering into the court process, both you and your former partner will have to deal with the delays that come with it. The time between lodging the application with the court and obtaining a final decision from a judge can be up to two years in Sydney. If you and your former partner cannot resolve the dispute yourselves, then the cost of the court process will be significant. Depending on the complexities of a dispute, a court hearing may cost each party between $30,000 and $250,000. A decision made by a judge will inevitably result in both you and your former partner losing the opportunity to come up with a creative and nuanced settlement deal yourselves. The judge will have a limited range of options available to him or her when the time comes to make a decision. The result is that often, judge-made decisions produce an outcome that neither party is happy with.

CHAPTER 6

TAKING A COMMERCIAL APPROACH

Chapter Summary

In this chapter we explain how, by taking into account commercial realities and managing your emotions, you can achieve a clever resolution at a much earlier stage in the separation process. The lessons to be discussed in this chapter are as follows:

Lesson 1—Understand What the Commercial Realities Are for You When You Are Negotiating a Family Dispute

Lesson 2—Find Out the Cost of All Available Options at the Very Beginning of the Process, and Compare That Cost to the Amount in Dispute

Lesson 3—At the Outset of the Process, Make a List of All the Interests You Will Need to Balance, and Keep That List at the Forefront of Your Mind throughout the Negotiations

Lesson 4—Remember That Happiness Is a Realistic and Achievable Goal, No Matter How Dark the Divorce Process Seems

LESSON 1

Understand What the Commercial Realities Are for You When You Are Negotiating a Family Dispute

What Is a Commercial Approach?

The definition of *commercial approach* differs in some significant aspects depending on whether the dispute is over the division of assets or the parenting of children.

In Relation to Division of Property

The term *commercial approach* is usually used in the context of disputes involving money. A business person owed money by a debtor has to take a commercial approach to recovering the debt. Usually that will mean weighing the costs of recovering the debt against the benefits of making the debtor pay. Typically, everything has to be reduced to a dollar value, including the total amount owed; the interest lost on the money owed; the fee paid to the debt-recovery agent or the solicitor to pursue the debt; the fees paid to a court or tribunal if there is a lawsuit; the fees paid to the other party if the court case is lost; the cost to the creditor regarding the time spent in pursuing the debtor; and whether the creditor can spend that time more effectively by attending to other business. Following a relationship breakdown, every case involving the division of assets is ultimately about dividing dollars. To that extent, the analysis of a commercial approach as set out above is just as applicable to a family property dispute as it is to a business seeking to recover a debt. Of course, the emotional stress and conflict associated with a relationship breakdown differentiates a dispute over the division of family assets from the recovery of a business debt. Therein lies the importance of the concept of a commercial approach to family property disputes. It is the very fact that emotional stress and conflict play such a significant part in these arguments that compels the adoption of a commercial approach as a circuit breaker to an ongoing dispute.

In adopting a commercial approach when negotiating the division of family assets, there are some key factors to be considered, for example:

- the total value of the joint net assets that you and your former partner are dividing;
- the primary "need" that you wish to satisfy from your settlement (for example, "I want to be able to buy a two-bedroom unit in Carlton." This has to be a genuine analysis, not something like, "I want as much as I can get");
- the amount of money you require to achieve the above goal, taking into account your borrowing capacity;
- regarding an argument over a percentage division of the total assets, how much a 1 per cent share is, and how far apart your percentage negotiations are in actual dollar terms;
- the amount your lawyer charges you per hour, and the cost of a one-day argument in court;
- how much have you spent on legal costs to date;
- how much money you may potentially spend on legal costs, and if this amount is disproportionate to the total value of the assets you are negotiating;
- how you would manage the stress arising from a drawn-out dispute over property division.

In Relation to Parenting

The term *commercial approach* in a parenting dispute has a very different meaning. When children are involved, it cannot be "just about the money." The commercial approach to parenting disputes is an approach that is focussed on the best interests of the children. *The best interests of the children* is a phrase that is often used but often misapplied. An obvious example is when both parents talk about wanting to protect the children's best interests but choose to become involved in a high-conflict court action to establish what those "best interests' are. The irony is that if the two parents were genuinely focussed on the best interests of the children, they would resolve all their differences, eliminate conflict, and devote all their attentions to parenting as a team. So commercial approach in relation to parenting is an approach that allows a parent to objectively identify a child's best interests and separate those interests from the parent's own wishes and preferences.

> **Example 1:** Jan has been the children's primary carer during her marriage. After their separation, Riley, her former partner, wants to share the care equally. Jan would prefer to stay in the role as primary carer, but she recognises that the equally shared care arrangement would work. Jan decides to put aside her own interests and agrees to the proposal in order to enable the children to have a strong continuing relationship with Riley in a conflict-free environment.

> **Example 2:** Ray, who was the secondary carer during his marriage, wants to slightly increase his involvement with the children now that he and his wife are separated. Joan, the primary carer, has a personality disorder and wishes to minimise contact between the children and their father. Ray has to choose between engaging in a long, drawn-out court battle, which might continue until the children are eighteen, or accepting the minimal time with the children that is proposed by Joan, which would minimise the long-term damage that continuing high conflict would inevitably bring to the children. Ray adopts a commercial approach to this situation and chooses to accept the minimal time he is offered with the children because he recognises that ongoing high conflict with Joan would cause too much long-term damage to the children. This is a difficult and courageous decision.

LESSON 2

Find Out the Cost of All Available Options at the Very Beginning of the Process, and Compare That Cost to the Amount in Dispute

What Does the Process Cost?

The process of dispute resolution can be divided into two separate alternatives. Parties can negotiate a resolution between themselves (with or without third-party assistance), or they can ask a court to impose a determination upon their case. The costs of these two alternatives are very different. When considering the total cost, you have to look at all the elements involved in that cost. The financial costs include not only the costs you pay your lawyer but also the fees you have to pay third parties such as expert witnesses. The non-financial costs include the stress of a prolonged dispute, the particularly high stress of a court hearing, and potential damage to relationships with children. We will simply examine the financial cost in this chapter.

A Negotiated Resolution

As we have seen earlier, a negotiated resolution can take different forms. The parties can talk through the issues and come up with their own solution by themselves, or the parties can negotiate through lawyers to reach an acceptable compromise. The latter option can involve a round-table conference between the parties and their respective lawyers at one lawyer's office, or the adoption of a collaborative law negotiation model. Parties can engage a professional mediator to help them reach an agreement, either with or without the involvement of their own lawyers. When it comes to the cost of resolving your dispute, all these negotiation options have two things in common. Firstly, you retain control over the outcome, and secondly, the cost of obtaining an acceptable final outcome is relatively low compared to the cost of court proceedings.

Mediators and lawyers will usually charge you an hourly rate for their services. A quality lawyer experienced in family law will charge between $300 and $600 per hour, depending on his or her background and geographical location. Even if you and your former partner resolve a dispute over the division of assets by yourselves, you will still have to visit a lawyer to have your agreement documented to comply with the Family Law Act and thereby become binding. You may expect that legal costs in this situation will be in the range of $3,000 to $5,000. If you and your former partner negotiate a resolution with the assistance of a mediator, then you will have to add the mediator's fee to the total cost of resolution. For a single day of mediation, the mediator's costs should be between $1,000 and $3,000. We should highlight that all of these figures are only basic guidelines, assuming that the parties have a limited range of assets. The costs in individual cases can vary wildly depending on the range of issues that are in dispute. Your own solicitor will provide you with a more precise fee estimate for your particular case.

A Court-Imposed Resolution

If a dispute goes all the way to a court hearing, the court process is always lengthy and costly. In Sydney, the time between commencing the court action and having a final hearing can be two years. This period varies from state to state and between different court offices. There is no standard measure of what a court action will cost, as the range of complicating factors in each individual case is almost infinite. In the most straightforward cases, each party can spend between $30,000 and $100,000 on legal costs after a full one-day hearing. Complicated cases can result in a party spending hundreds of thousands of dollars on legal costs. In addition, each party will have to pay costs for third parties involved in the court dispute. These third parties can include property valuers, forensic accountants to value business structures, psychologists to assess parties and children, and doctors to provide medical reports. These third parties, because they provide evidence to support your case, requirement payment for their time spent in preparing a report and their time to attend court to provide evidence, if so required. In simple cases, the third-party expert will cost between $5,000 and $15,000 to prepare a report and to attend court to give evidence on your behalf. Often the court orders that the costs of these third-party experts be shared between the parties. In most straightforward disputes, the legal costs and expenses of proceeding to seek a court-imposed outcome can be out of proportion to the total value of the assets in dispute.

> **Example:** Vince and Donna have a home worth $1,000,000, a mortgage of $500,000, and a superannuation fund of $150,000, meaning that the total net value of the assets they own is $650,000. Vince claims 50 per cent of the asset pool, but Donna wants to give him only 40 per cent of the asset pool. Their dispute is over 10 per cent of the asset pool, or $65,000. If they cannot resolve the dispute and instead choose to go to court, then, in this relatively simple matter, they will each spend about $50,000 on legal costs. The lack of proportionality between the amount in dispute, $65,000, and the total costs of arguing, $100,000, is obvious, so they agree that Vince will receive 45 per cent of the asset pool.

LESSON 3

At the Outset of the Process, Make a List of All the Interests You Will Need to Balance, and Keep That List at the Forefront of Your Mind throughout the Negotiations

What Interests Do You Need to Balance?

When considering your options in a family law negotiation, you should take into account several important issues, as follows:

The Cost of a Dispute

When you are involved in a dispute following a family breakdown, it is very important to keep an eye on the amount you have spent and will spend on legal and other costs. That may sound like an obvious statement, but the question of cost is often overlooked, or overtaken by the emotion stemming from the dispute itself. A good lawyer will ensure that you are fully aware of the costs you are incurring in the context of the negotiations you are undertaking, and keep you focussed on the proportionality referred to previously in this chapter.

The Risk of a Judge-Imposed Decision

The beauty of a negotiated resolution is that you and your former partner have control over the outcome. While the outcome may be a compromise, it is a compromise that you have structured, meaning that you have crafted a solution that works for you both. When you go to court and the judge has to make the decision, the actual decision and the structure of the result is outside your control. This may mean that the judge will make a decision that incorporates features that are totally at odds with what you had hoped for.

> **Example:** Dan made an application to the court for an order that would enable him to retain the house by

buying out Phillippa's interest. He argued that Phillippa was entitled to only 40 per cent of value of the house. The former partners, unable to resolve the matter, went to a court hearing. The judge decided that the house would be sold and that 50 per cent of the proceeds would be paid to each party. Dan could have afforded to buy out Phillippa's interest and paid her 50 per cent of the value of the property, but he chose not to take that route. The judge's decision, and the legal costs incurred by Dan in that court action, made it so that Dan has lost the opportunity to buy out Phillippa's interest and is rendered unable to retain the house.

Your Long-Term Financial Future

Any decisions you make about the settlement of a financial dispute must be based on the long-term impact of such decisions. Too often we have seen people focussed on the short-term benefits at the expense of their longer-term security. A party may be so focussed on retaining their home at any cost that they give up significant entitlements or incur too much debt to achieve long-term security. A party may fail to understand their longer-term financial needs and choose to give up too much just to finalise the dispute. A party may decide to trade off a superannuation fund and take a smaller overall percentage of the assets in order to gain access to the liquid assets because he or she feels that he or she needs the cash now. A party may continue the dispute over relatively small amounts of money as a matter of principle. Because you only get one shot at family law property division, you must always keep focussed on the main game—to set yourself up financially for your long-term future.

Your Ongoing Relationship with Your Children

When you are caught up in arguments over parenting arrangements, it is often easy to focus on the short-term issues, such as demanding that the children be returned on a particular weekend at 5:00 p.m. instead of at 5:45 p.m. Raising children is a long-term commitment. We always remind our clients of the importance of maintaining a quality lifelong relationship with their children so that they can celebrate the great moments in life with them—their twenty-first birthday, their graduation from university, their marriage, or the birth of their first child. Often, a drawn-out, high-conflict parenting dispute can have serious negative effects on children. The risk of this is that the parent–child relationship becomes damaged for the longer term as a result. A compromise that limits your time with your child in the short term and puts an end to a damaging conflict can result, as your child matures, in that child's developing an understanding of the role you played in ending the conflict. This, in turn, can result in a much closer relationship between you and your child in his or her later life. We have met some people who, with great courage, gave up the fight for their children because they saw the conflict with their partner as having a much more negative impact on the children than did the compromise that limited the parent's time with the children in the short term. These people have, without fail, gone on to have strong, meaningful, and happy relationships with their children later in life.

The Emotional and Physical Impact of a Drawn-Out Dispute

One of the least understood aspects of a family law dispute is the impact it will have on your emotional and physical health. While it is clear that the end of a relationship can be an horrendously stressful and emotionally turbulent time, the effect on your well-being caused by the breakdown itself can pale in significance when compared to the worry and pressure that arises after a legal dispute is commenced. All the stressors are amplified, because the legal process, by its very nature, is confrontational and promotes antagonism. As a result, the longer a dispute extends, the more confrontational it becomes and the more painful the experience is. There is no better example of this than when parties are compelled to set out in affidavits all the factors that entitle them to a greater share of the property or all the factors that make them a better parent than their former partner. Those affidavits contain very personal and, often, very hurtful material. The pressure and worry is stepped up to another level if you become involved in a court hearing and have to be cross-examined in the witness box. Dealing with a skilled barrister in that situation is terrifying at best. Many people have described the experience as making them feel totally worthless. We have seen instances where people have, in the face of difficult court proceedings, had their relationships with friends and family adversely affected by the pressure. In the worst cases, those involved in court disputes have had to deal with severe depressive episodes or physical illnesses.

LESSON 4

Remember That Happiness Is a Realistic and Achievable Goal, No Matter How Dark the Divorce Process Seems

The Joy of a New Start

We have lost count of the number of times clients have said to us, at some stage after the conclusion of their family law dispute, "I am really happy." The painful process of ending a relationship does not reach a formal conclusion until the property division and parenting issues are resolved. Up to that point, you will continue to be weighed down by the grief, the anger, the stress, and/or the frustration of dealing with your former partner. Those feelings are perfectly normal during this process, but the longer the process continues, the longer the period of emotional pain you will experience. Once the family law dispute is finalised, however, you will have a new perspective on your own future, and typically that perspective is very positive. You will contemplate to yourself, or hear from your friends, the following things:

- "Why didn't you do this years ago?"
- "You seem much happier."
- "You now control your own destiny."
- "I can do what I always wanted to do."
- "You look better and healthier."
- "I love the independence."

Without doubt, a new start at the end of a relationship can carry with it certain financial constraints. But again, typically, those constraints are manageable and will not interfere with your ability to experience the extraordinary emotional benefits of your new-found independence. You should not underestimate these benefits, even though it is difficult even to think of them during a family law dispute. They are very real and can result in your becoming a much better person than even you thought possible.

CHAPTER 7

THE BEST WAY TO RESOLVE A FAMILY LAW PROPERTY DISPUTE—A CASE STUDY

Chapter Summary

In this chapter, we provide you with a case study, and the best way to resolve your dispute by applying the guidelines set out in *Watkins Tapsell's Guide to Separation and Family Law*. The lessons to be discussed in this chapter are as follows:

Lesson 1—If You and Your Former Partner Are Able to Work Together to Find a Solution, Then You Can Reach an Agreement between Yourselves and Take That Agreement to Your Lawyers for Formalisation with the Court

Lesson 2—If You Instruct a Competent Lawyer to Negotiate on Your Behalf, the Dispute Can Progress to a Resolution More Quickly and Efficiently

Lesson 3—If You Can't Reach Agreement between Yourselves, or with the Help of Your Lawyers, It May Assist to Bring in a Neutral Third Party (Like a Mediator). The Mediator Can Provide Insights into the Other Party's Motivations and Thereby Assist in Resolving the Dispute

Lesson 4—Sometimes Commencing Court Proceedings Is the Best Option to Progress Your Dispute, Such as When Your Former Partner Refuses to Communicate or Negotiate. Commencing Court Proceedings Can Be a Useful Tool to Assist You in Reaching a Negotiated Resolution

Lesson 5—Implementing Your Agreement by Using Formal Court Orders, Made by Consent, Guarantees That You Achieve Finality and Minimise Any Stamp Duty or Capital Gains Tax

The Case Study Background

Graham and Sarah were married for twenty years. When they were first married, they did not have any significant assets or savings. They now have two children, aged eleven and seventeen. During their marriage, Graham has worked full time and Sarah has looked after the children. Sarah also worked part time in the early part of the marriage. Both Graham and Sarah have always applied their incomes to the needs of the family. Now that they have separated, Sarah would like to continue in her role as primary carer to the children, but she also supports and encourages the children in spending time with Graham. Graham is fifty-five years old and is hoping to retire by age sixty. He has a good superannuation pension plan and would like to keep his superannuation intact. Sarah is forty-five years old and has returned to full-time work now that both children are older. She wants to stay in the family home with the children. She has gone to see a lawyer, whom she told that she wants to resolve the dispute quickly and cheaply, and that she still wants to be friends with Graham afterwards.

LESSON 1

If You and Your Former Partner Are Able to Work Together to Find a Solution, Then You Can Reach an Agreement between Yourselves and Take That Agreement to Your Lawyers for Formalisation with the Court

Graham and Sarah have the following assets and liabilities:

Asset	Ownership	Value
House	Joint	$1,000,000
Car	Graham	$10,000
Car	Sarah	$20,000
Shares	Joint	$150,000
Savings	Joint	$50,000
Subtotal assets		$1,230,000
Liabilities	Ownership	Value
Mortgage	Joint	-$200,000
Credit card	Joint	-$10,000
Subtotal liabilities		-$210,000
Superannuation fund	Ownership	Value
	Graham	$600,000
	Sarah	$150,000
Subtotal superannuation fund		$750,000
Total (net) assets		$1,770,000

Negotiations between Parties to the Relationship

The first thing Sarah did was make an appointment to see her lawyer (see chapter 2, under "Choosing the Right Lawyer"). Before meeting with her lawyer, Sarah asked her lawyer what documents she should bring with her to the appointment. The lawyer sent Sarah some information, and Sarah was able to gather together the material to hand to her lawyer in that first meeting (see chapter 2, under "Preparation"). At that first meeting, Sarah's lawyer explained to her the formula for dividing property (see chapter 2, under "What Is the Formula for Dividing Property?"). After meeting with Sarah and having an opportunity to review the material, Sarah's lawyer was able to provide her with an initial assessment of her entitlement and give her some guidance on constructive offers. Sarah's lawyer also gave her some options for dividing the asset pool in a way that suited Sarah's needs. Sarah, who had an amicable relationship with Graham, arranged a meeting with him to try to work out with him what they wanted to do with their assets (see chapter 3, under "Sorting It Out Yourselves").

LESSON 2

If You Instruct a Competent Lawyer to Negotiate on Your Behalf, Reasonable Offers Can Be Made and the Dispute Can Often Progress to Resolution More Quickly and Efficiently

Negotiations through Lawyers

Unfortunately, Graham and Sarah were not able to work out a final agreement between themselves. Both Graham and Sarah instructed their respective lawyers to try to resolve their dispute (see chapter 3, under "Negotiations between Lawyers"). The first thing Sarah's lawyer did was to gather all of Sarah's financial disclosure material (see chapter 3, under "Disclosure"). Sarah's lawyer then worked with Graham's lawyer to exchange each party's financial material. Once all of that material had been exchanged, both lawyers formed a view of the case and provided their respective clients with advice. Each party made formal offers of settlement by letter. The offers made by the lawyers were thorough and reasonable. Because both lawyers made clear offers that were supported by the disclosure material their clients had given them, the issues were quickly narrowed (the fewer issues the parties are fighting over, the greater the chance they have of resolving their dispute). The lawyers, along with Graham and Sarah, met at Sarah's lawyer's office to discuss how to reach a final resolution.

LESSON 3

If You Can't Reach Agreement between Yourselves or with the Help of Your Lawyers, It May Assist to Bring in a Neutral Third Party (Like a Mediator). The Mediator Can Provide Insights into the Other Party's Motivations and Thereby Assist in Resolving the Dispute

Negotiations Using a Mediator

Unfortunately Sarah and Graham were not able to resolve their dispute with the assistance of their lawyers. Sarah's lawyer believed that Sarah and her former partner were close to a resolution and recommended to Sarah that the former partners appoint a mediator and attend mediation in an effort to resolve the dispute. Sarah's lawyer assessed the matter and made a recommendation to Sarah about an appropriate mediator (see chapter 3, under "Mediation without Lawyers"). Graham's lawyer and Sarah's lawyer each prepared a summary of their respective client's claim for the mediator, which set out the basis of their case and the history of the relationship. The summary gave the mediator a full and thorough understanding of the issues in dispute. Graham and Sarah then met with the mediator without their lawyers. Through the mediation process, the mediator spoke to Sarah, who told him that she desperately wanted to keep the house and stay there with the kids. The mediator also spoke to Graham, who told him that he really wanted to keep his superannuation fund and pension intact, saying that if that happened, he would also need a little extra money to rehouse because he would not be able to access his superannuation fund for another five years. The mediator was then able to guide Sarah and Graham to a resolution that allowed Sarah to keep the house (with a small mortgage that she could maintain now that she had returned to full-time work) and allowed Graham to keep his superannuation fund plus some savings, and some shares that he could sell (which gave him funds towards his rehousing costs).

LESSON 4

Sometimes Commencing Court Proceedings
Is the Best Option to Progress a Dispute,
Such as When Your Former Partner Refuses to
Communicate or Negotiate. Commencing
Court Proceedings Can Be a Useful Tool to Assist
You in Reaching a Negotiated Resolution

The Court Option

Let's assume that Sarah and Graham were not able to resolve their dispute by any of the aforementioned methods. Their next option is to commence court proceedings. Initially, Graham refused to negotiate or to communicate and did not want to accept that the relationship was over. Sarah accepted advice that commencing proceedings was the only way of forcing Graham to deal with the matter (see chapter 5, under "When Will Court Proceedings Be Necessary?"). Sarah commenced court proceedings in family court as a means of persuading Graham to resolve the dispute. She understood that the family court system is designed to encourage settlement between parties at every opportunity. The first two times that Sarah and Graham went to court, they attended a private session in a court officer's office. The second of these sessions was a conciliation conference (which is essentially a settlement conference where the court officer works together with the parties and their lawyers to try to resolve the dispute). Graham, although not willing to negotiate reasonably at the beginning, was forced to listen to the court officer, who explained very clearly the advantages of resolving the dispute by settlement. Graham recognised that the court officer knew what he was talking about, and was worried when the court officer said Graham was being unrealistic. Graham and Sarah reached agreement at the conciliation conference, and the solicitors immediately prepared court consent orders. Graham and Sarah signed the consent orders, and the court officer made the orders on the spot. Graham and Sarah left the court knowing that their whole dispute had been finalised (see chapter 4, under "Court Consent Orders").

LESSON 5

Implementing Your Agreement by Using Formal Court Orders, Made by Consent, Guarantees That You Achieve Finality and Minimise Any Stamp Duty or Capital Gains Tax

Implementation

Whenever an agreement is reached, the next step is to implement it. Sarah and Graham had documented their agreement very carefully in their court orders. Now their agreement had to be physically implemented. In our case study, Sarah and Graham reached an agreement to divide their assets equally, as shown in the following table:

Asset	Sarah	Graham
House	$1,000,000	
Car		$10,000
Car	$20,000	
Shares		$150,000
Savings		$50,000
Subtotal assets	$1,020,000	$210,000
Liabilities	Sarah	Graham
Mortgage	-$200,000	
Credit card		-$10,000
Subtotal liabilities	-$200,000	-$10,000
Superannuation fund	Sarah	Graham
		$600,000
	65,000	$85,000
Subtotal superannuation	$65,000	$685,000
Total (net) assets split equally	$885,000	$885,000

The former partners achieved this outcome by agreeing that Graham would transfer his interest in the house to Sarah, while Sarah would take over sole responsibility for the mortgage. They would each keep their own car, and Graham would retain the shares and savings, which he could later use as a deposit for a new house. Graham would also retain his entire superannuation fund and would receive $85,000 of Sarah's superannuation fund. If they had not already drafted and signed court consent orders at their court conference, then Graham would have arranged for his lawyer to draft consent orders and send them to Sarah's lawyer. Once both parties were happy that the terms of the written document were consistent with their agreement, they would both sign and one of their lawyers would then lodge the court orders in the court. Two weeks later, the court would issue the sealed consent orders, and from that point on, neither party could alter the agreement.

The lawyers then proceed to implement Graham and Sarah's agreement. Graham signed a document to transfer his interest in the house to Sarah. There was no stamp duty payable on that transfer because it was a transfer pursuant to court orders. Sarah applied to the bank for a new loan to refinance the mortgage so that the new mortgage would be in her sole name. Graham was no longer liable for any of the mortgage debt. Sarah signed share transfers and bank documents to transfer her interest in the shares and cash savings to Graham. There was no capital gains tax payable on the share transfers because they were pursuant to court orders. Graham took over payment of the credit card debt. Graham's lawyer sent a copy of the court orders to the trustee of Sarah's superannuation fund, and the trustee then split Sarah's superannuation fund and transferred part of it, $85,000, to Graham's superannuation account.

CONCLUSION

The difficulty of resolving a family law dispute over the division of property and/or parenting issues should never be underestimated. There are, however, steps you can take that will help you to navigate the minefield that is divorce. Those steps can save you a significant amount of money and substantially ease the emotional stress and turmoil you would otherwise suffer.

We hope that *Watkins Tapsell's Guide to Separation and Family Law* has provided you with the tools to help identify those steps and to enable you to make the difficult decisions aimed at achieving a sensible resolution.

ABOUT THE AUTHOR

Matthew Coates is a partner at the law firm Watkins Tapsell and has been pracitising family law in Sydney, Australia, since 1980. He has experienced the difficulties faced by ordinary people as they go through divorce, which inspired him to write this book. He lives in Southern Sydney with his wife and two daughters and enjoys golf, playing guitars, and singing.

Kristy Durrant is a partner at Watkins Tapsell and an accredited specialist in family law. She has been practising law since 2004 and is a trained mediator. She formerly was a primary school teacher and worked as a lawyer with the Department of Education. She lives with her husband and three children in Southern Sydney.

Jamie Roche is a partner at Watkins Tapsell. He began his law career in 2002 in the United States and is a member of the bar in Massachusetts and New Hampshire. He is now practising law in Australia. Throughout his career, he has practised extensively in family law, and he is an accredited mediator. He lives in Southern Sydney with his wife and two sons.

Printed in the United States
By Bookmasters